Jewishness

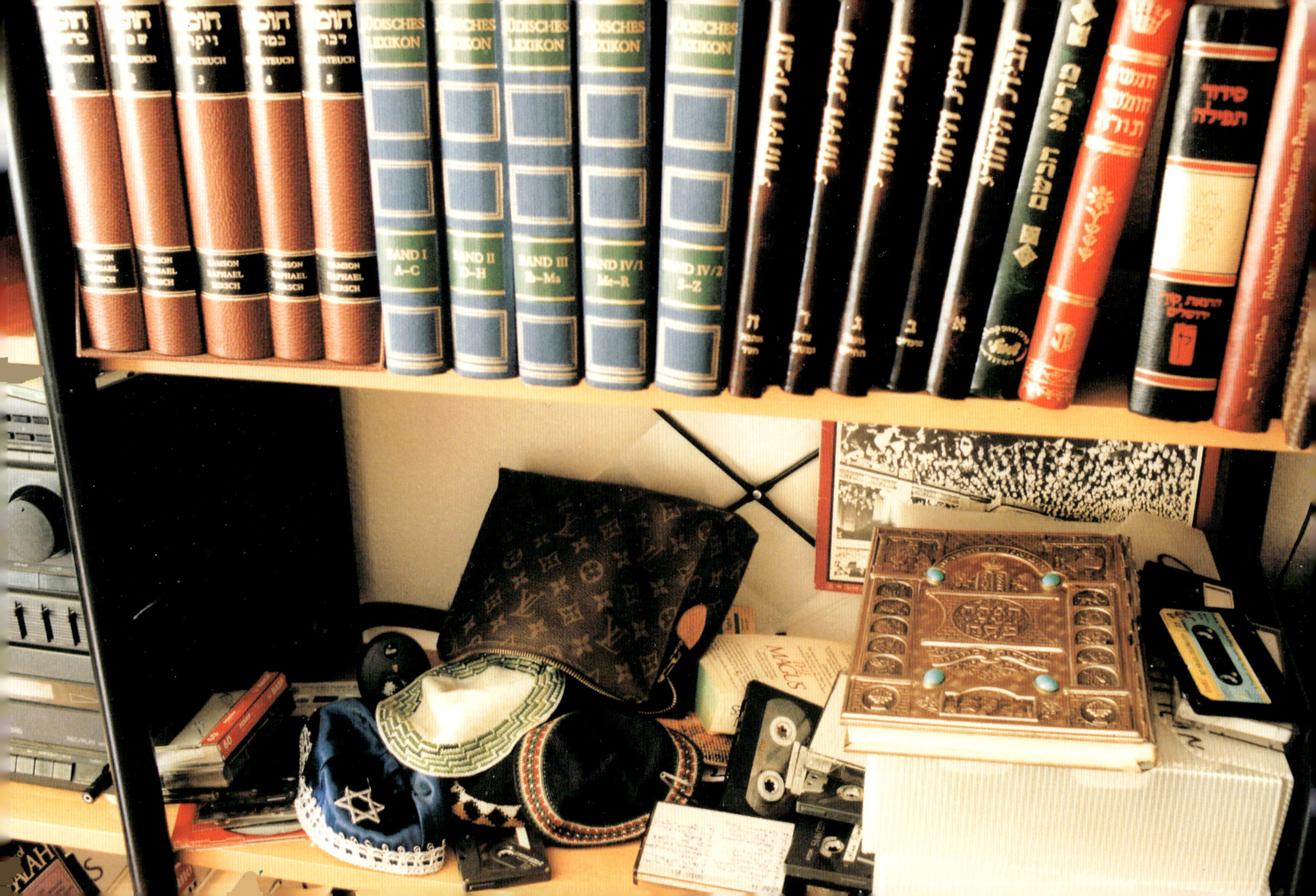

Peter Loewy

Jewishness

Gina Kehayoff

Munich

For my parents

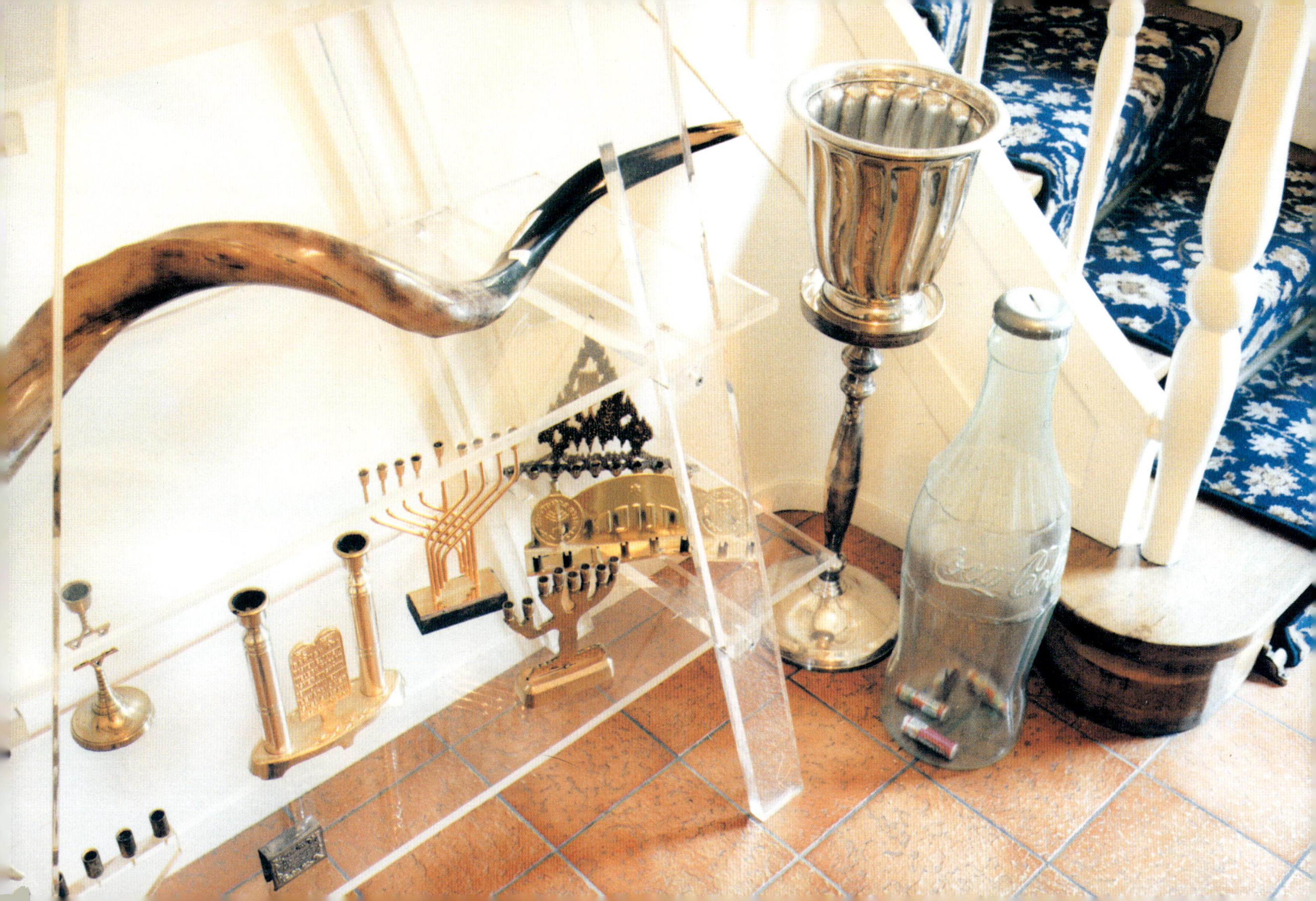

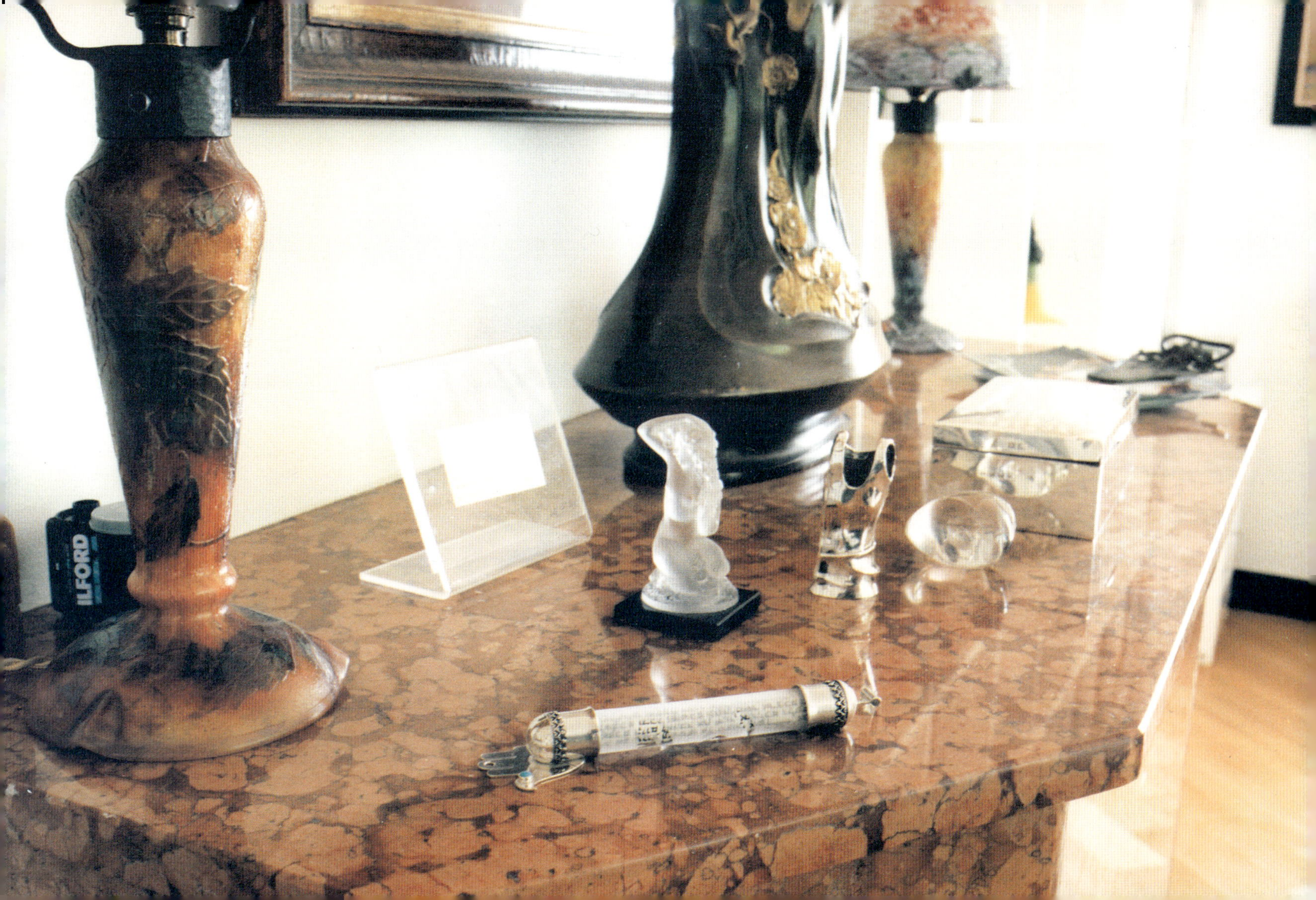

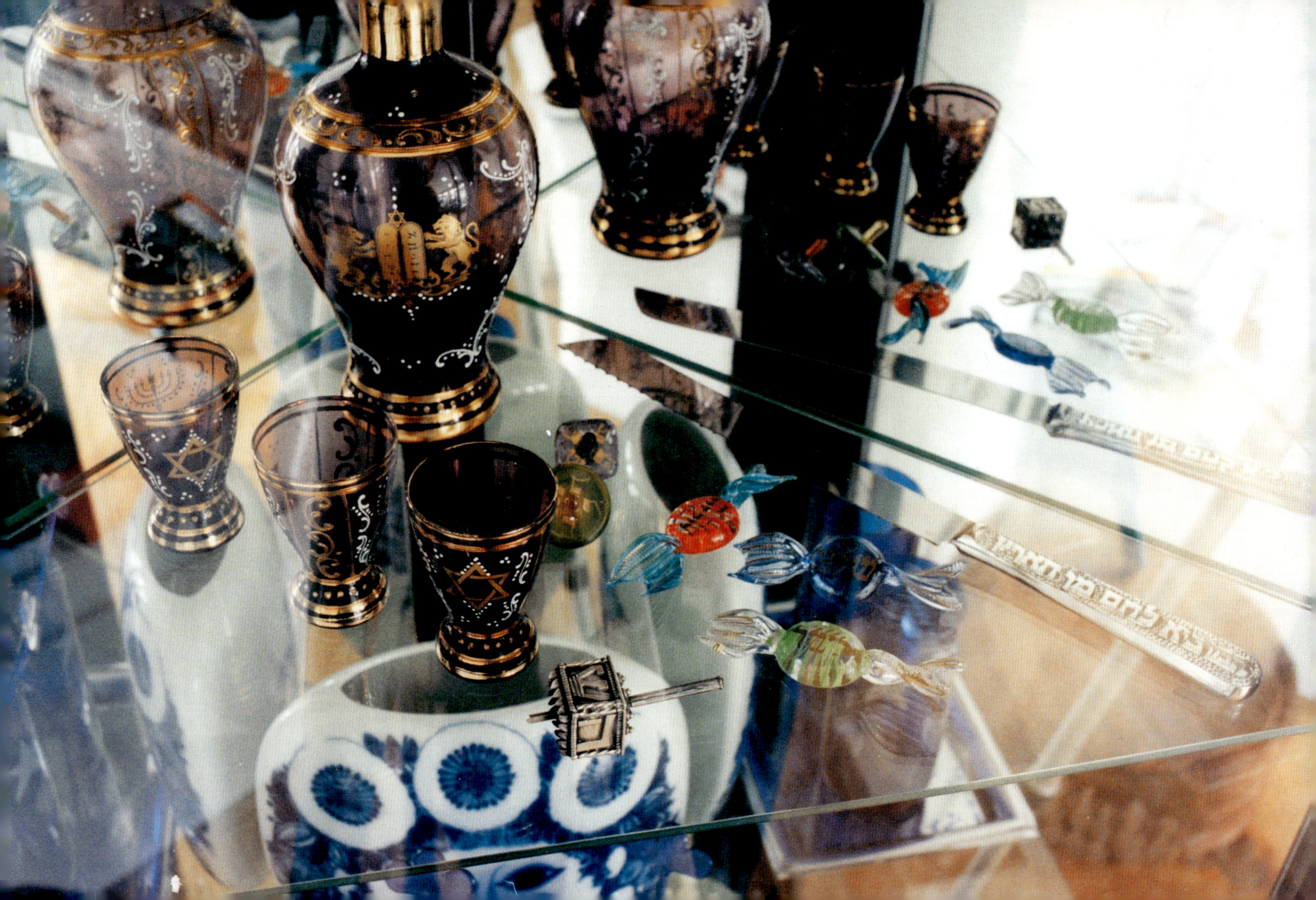

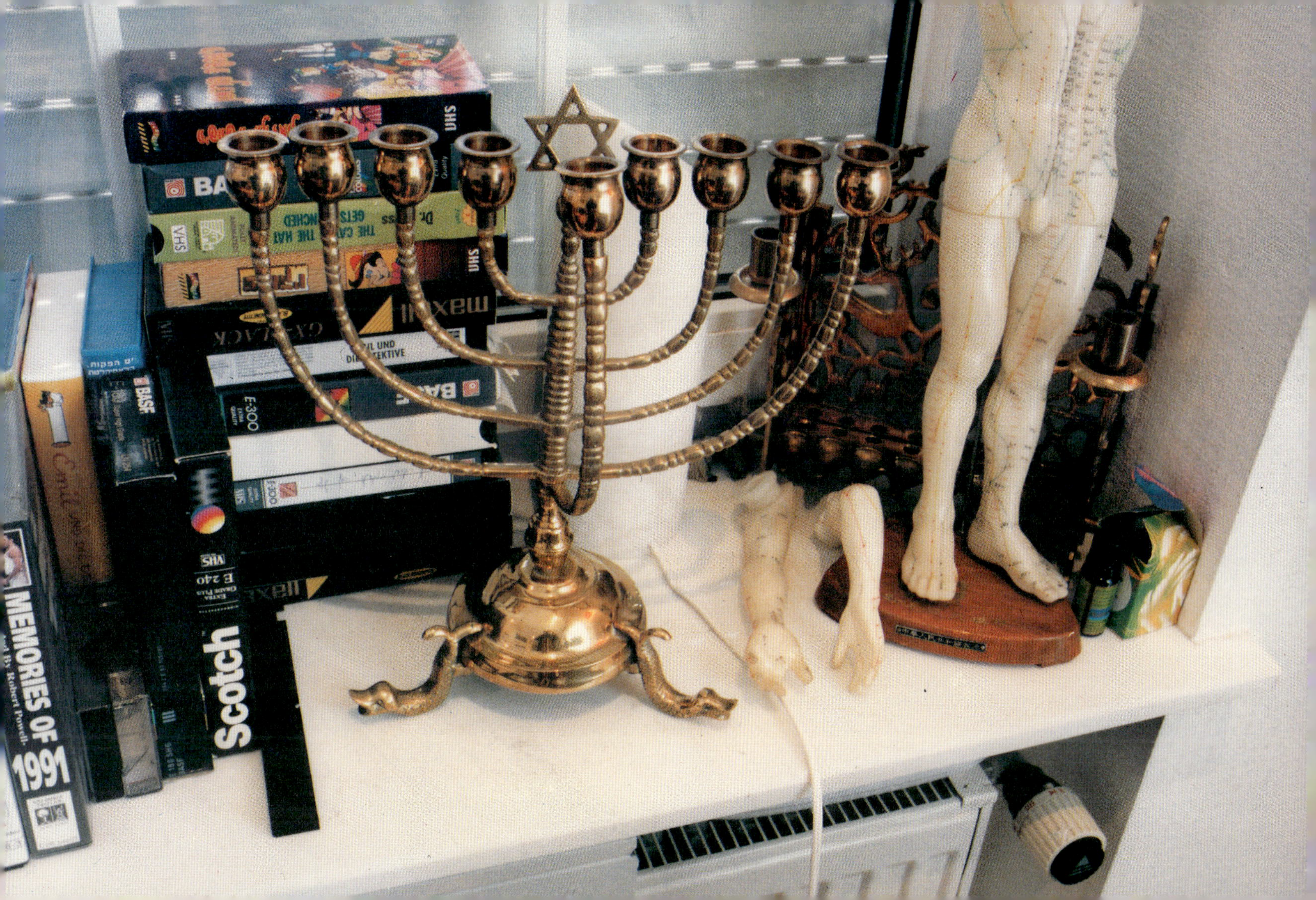
UHS
BASF
THE CAT IN THE HAT GETS PINCHED
VHS
maxell
GX-PACK
DER DETEKTIVE
BASF
E-300
E-300
VHS
maxell
E 240
Scotch
E 240
MEMORIES OF 91
By Robert Powell
1991

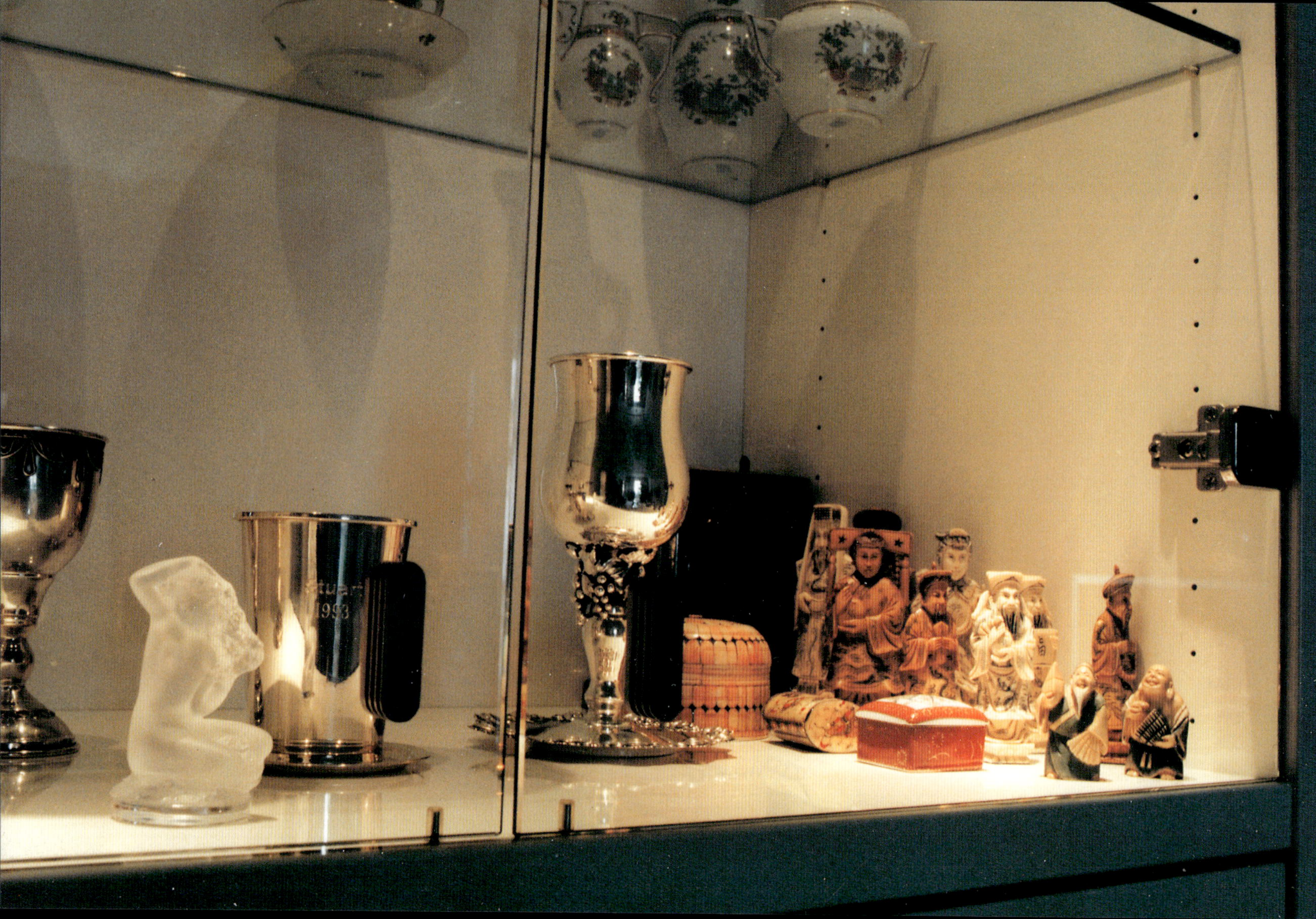

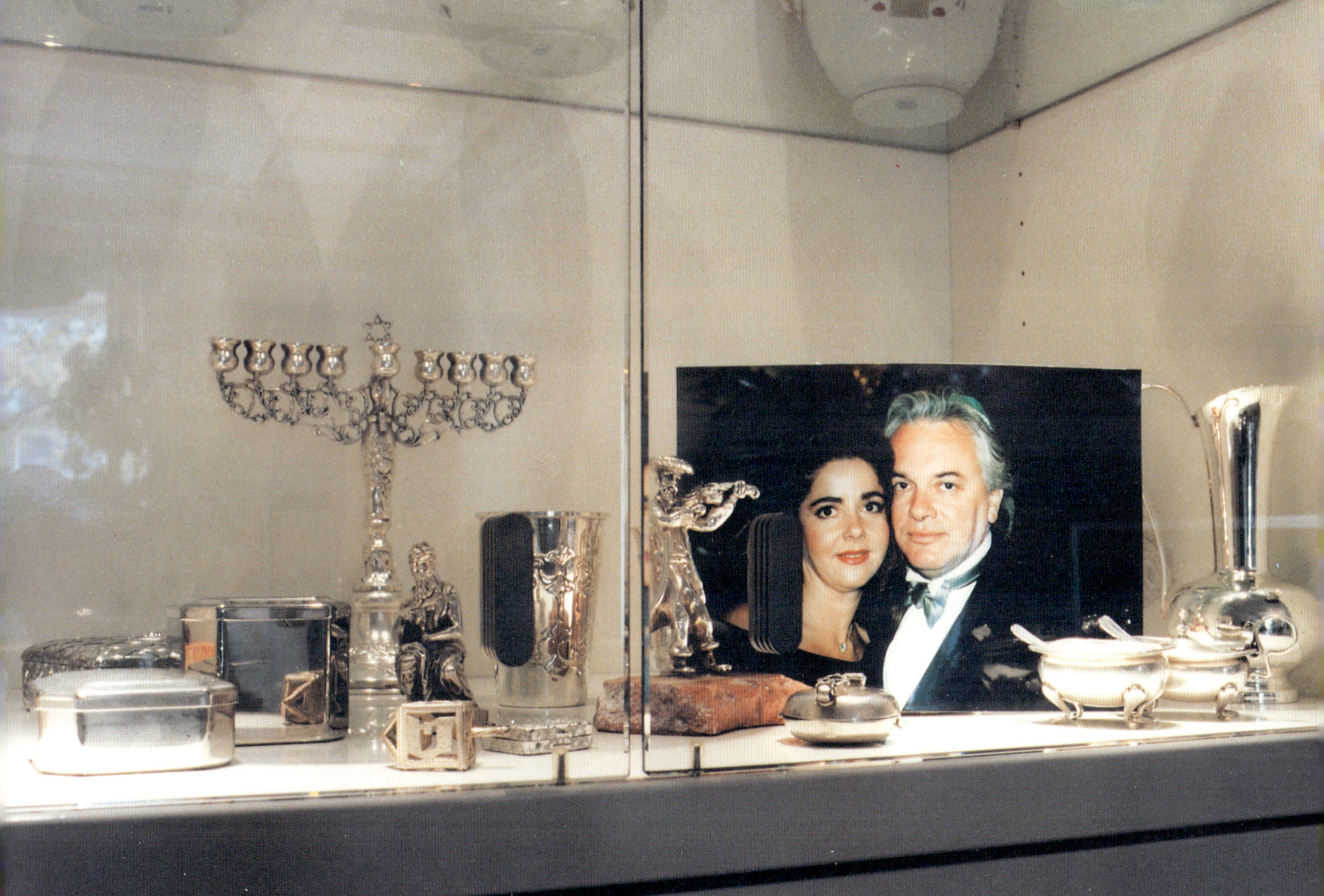

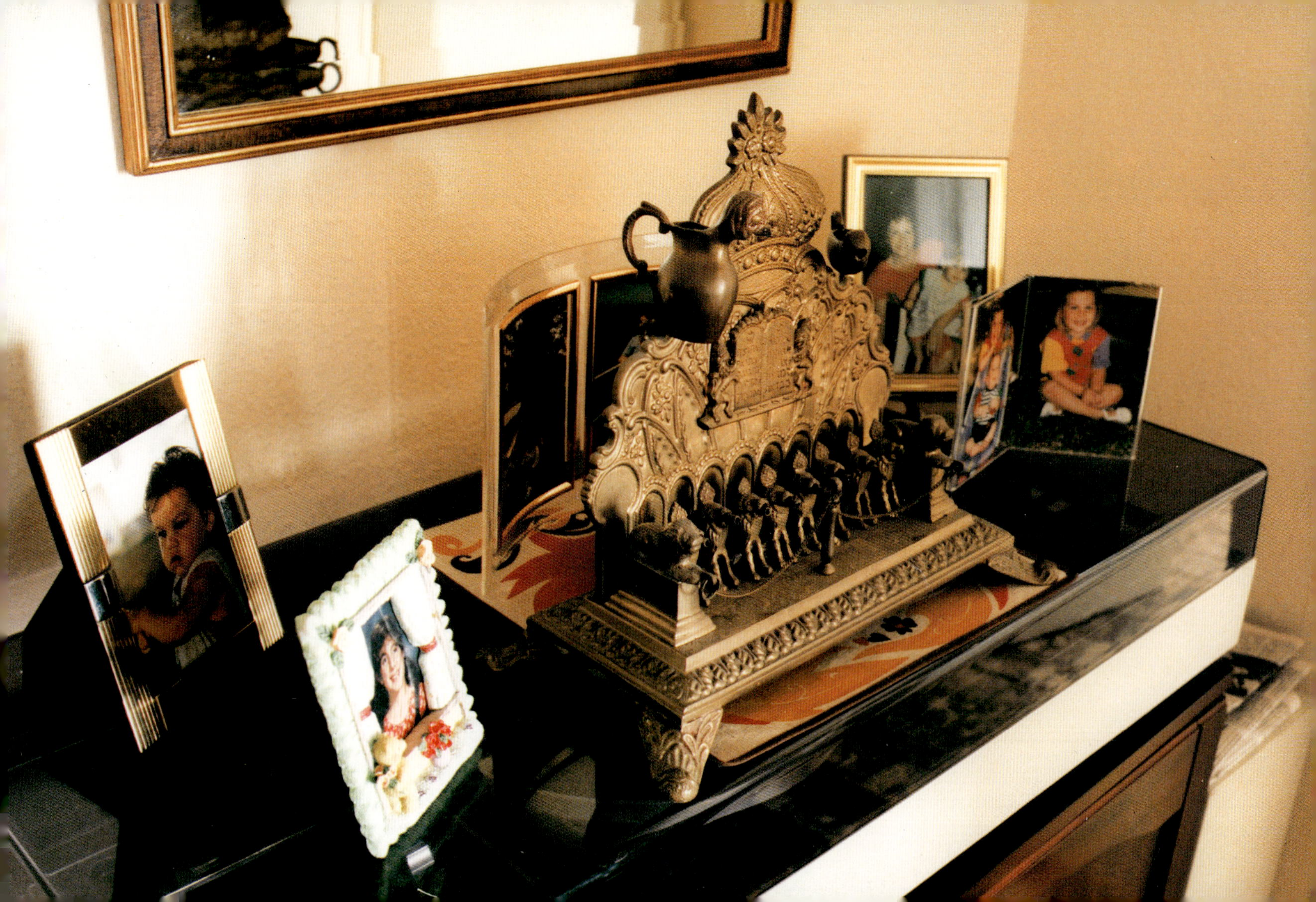

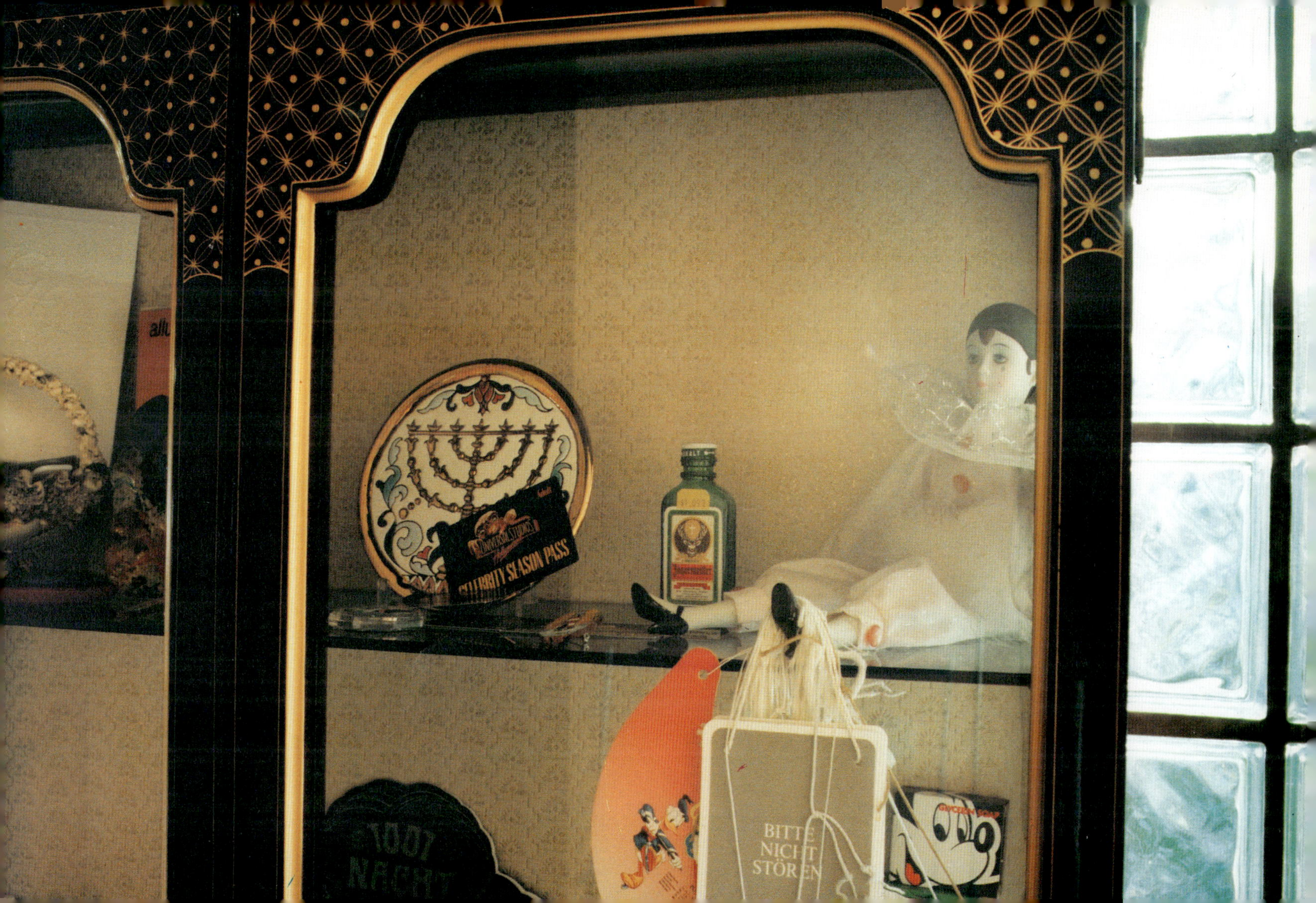
allu
UNIVERSAL STUDIOS
CELEBRITY SEASON PASS
1001
NACHT
BITTE
NICHT
STÖREN

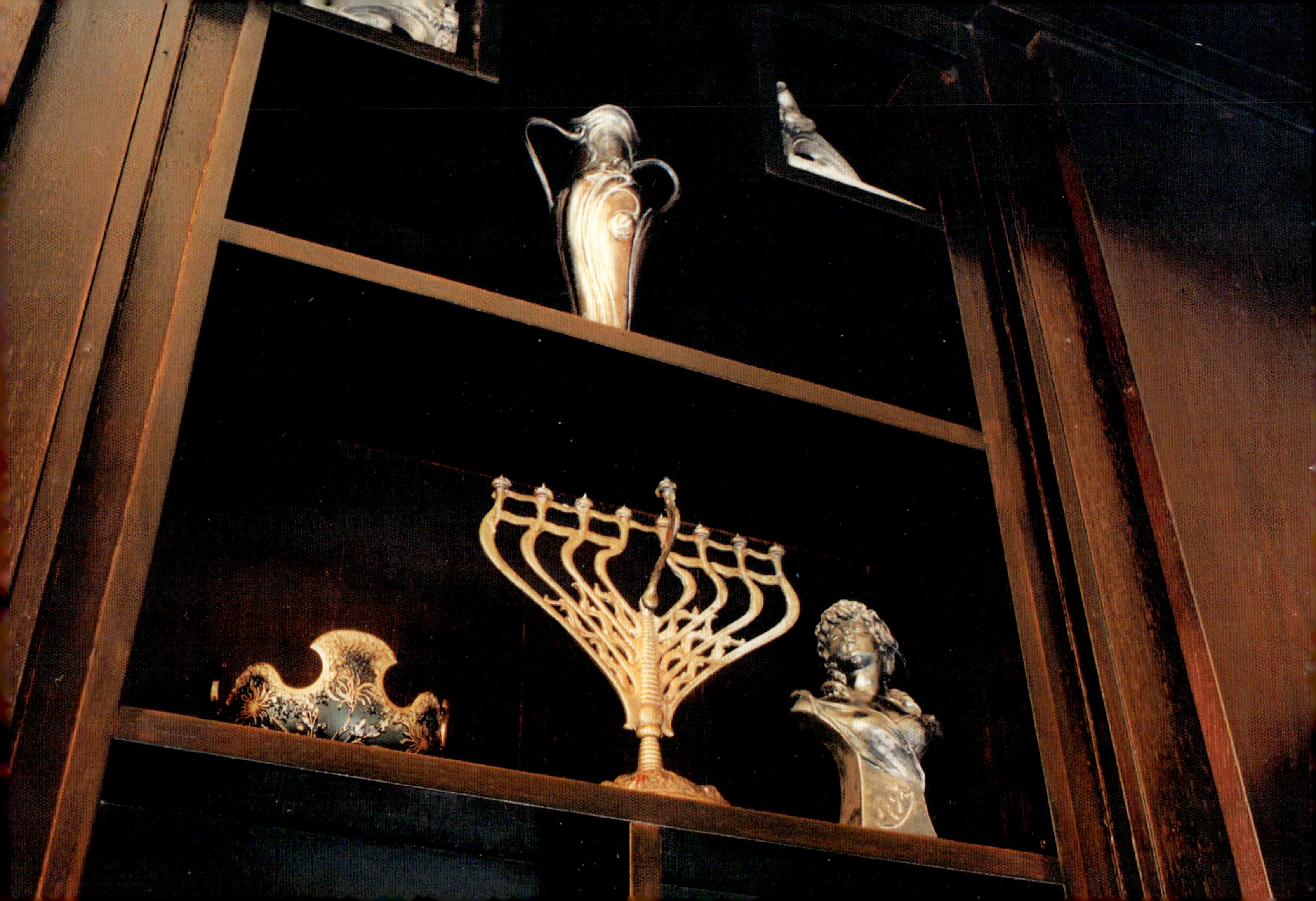

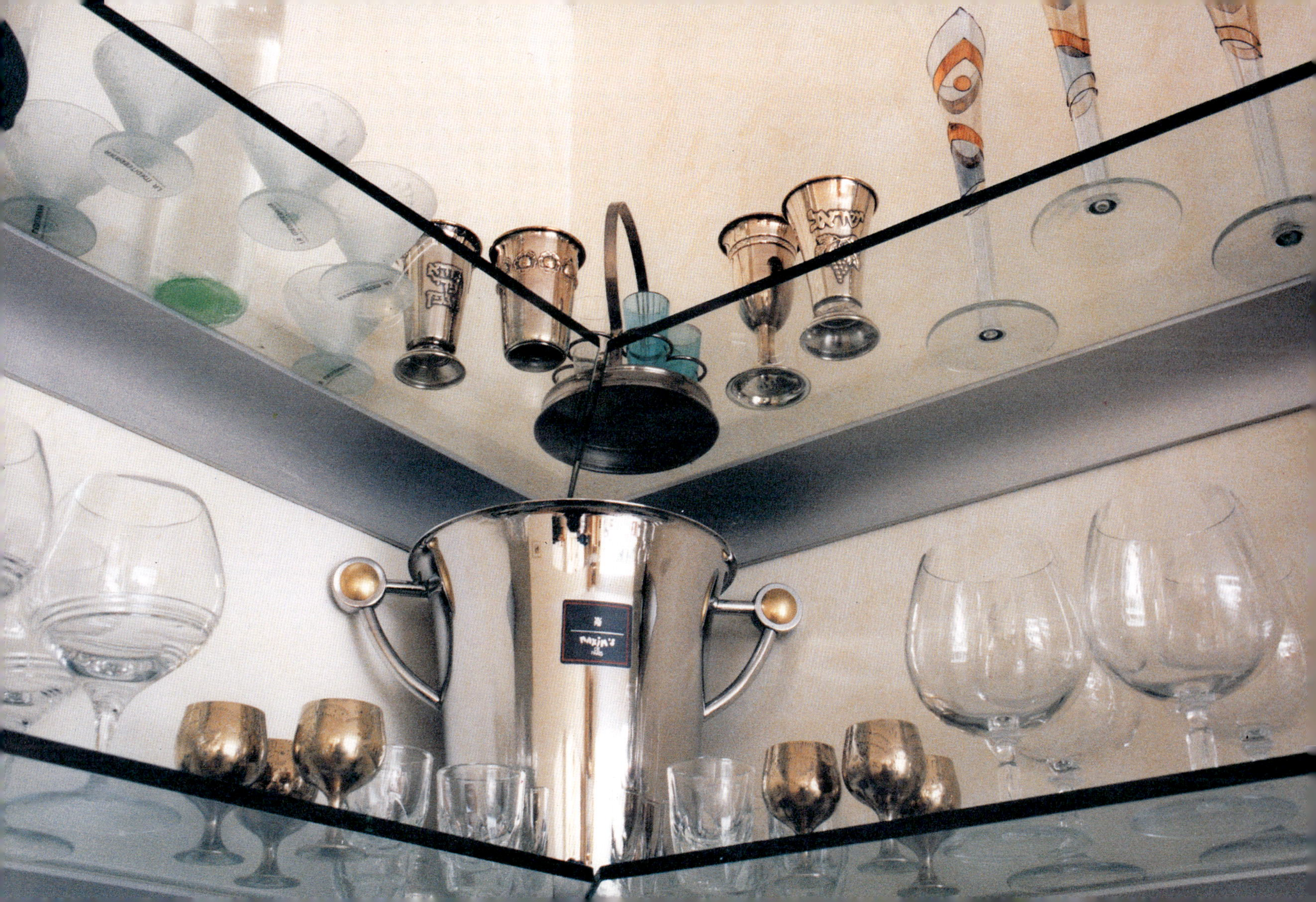

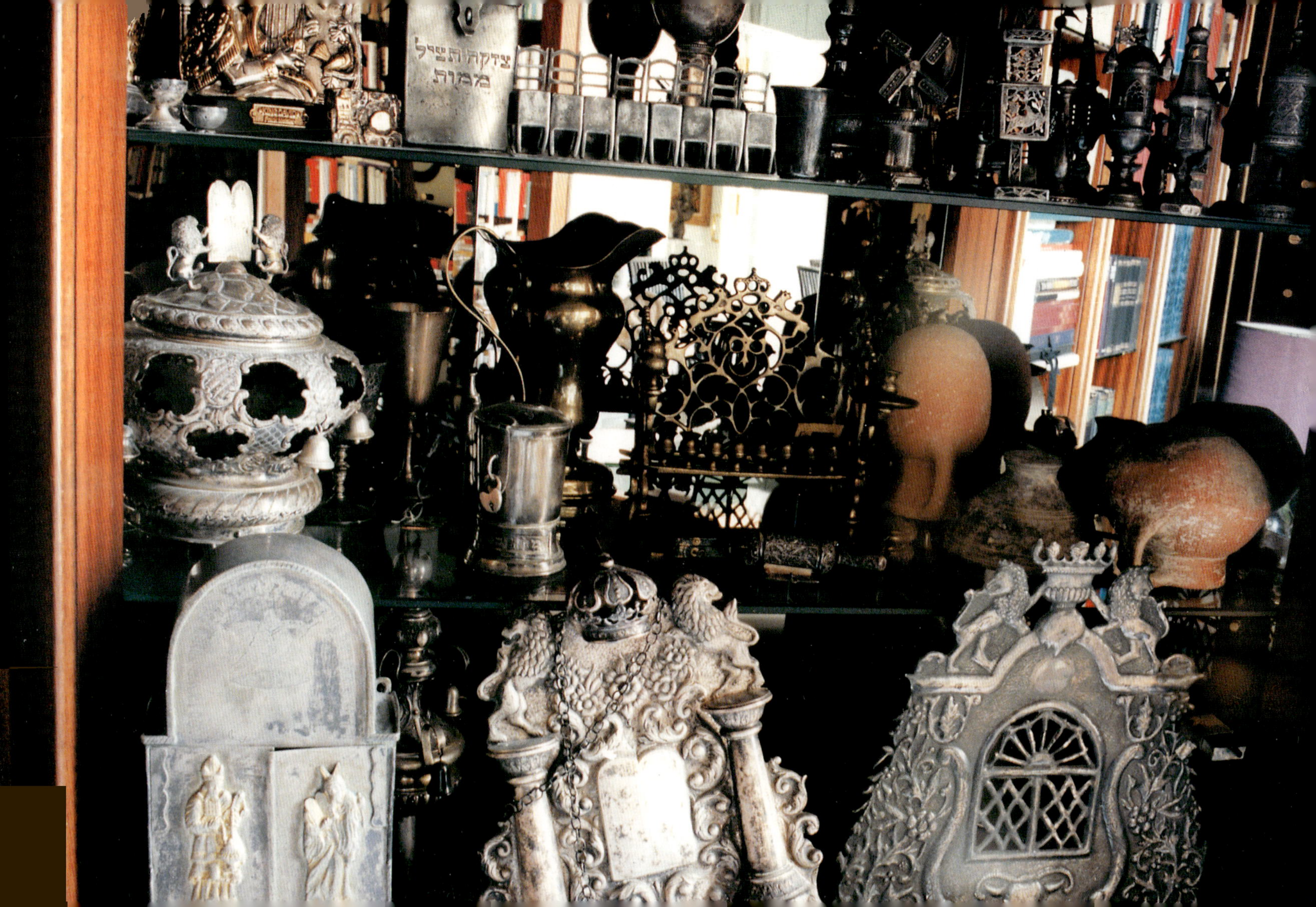

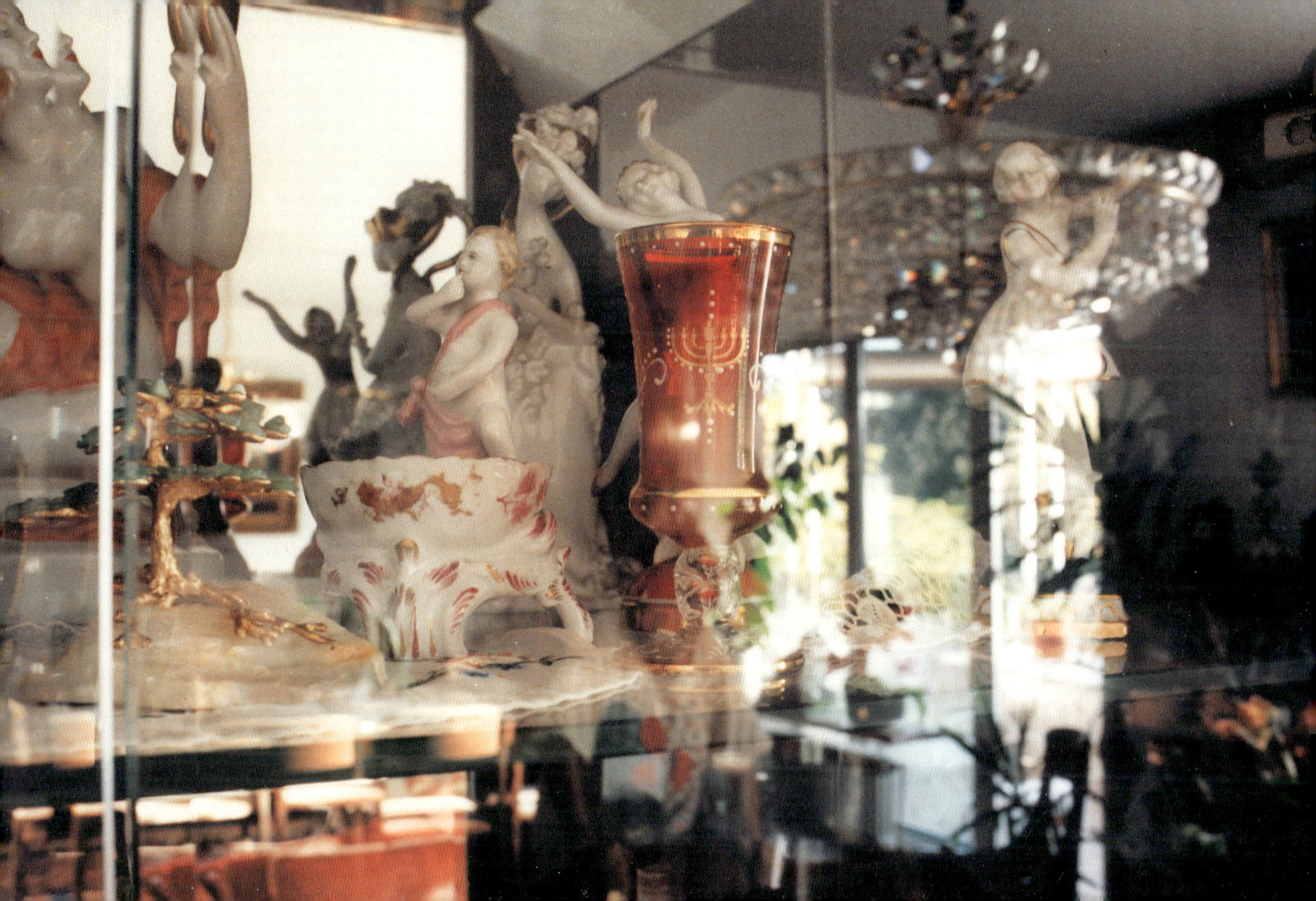

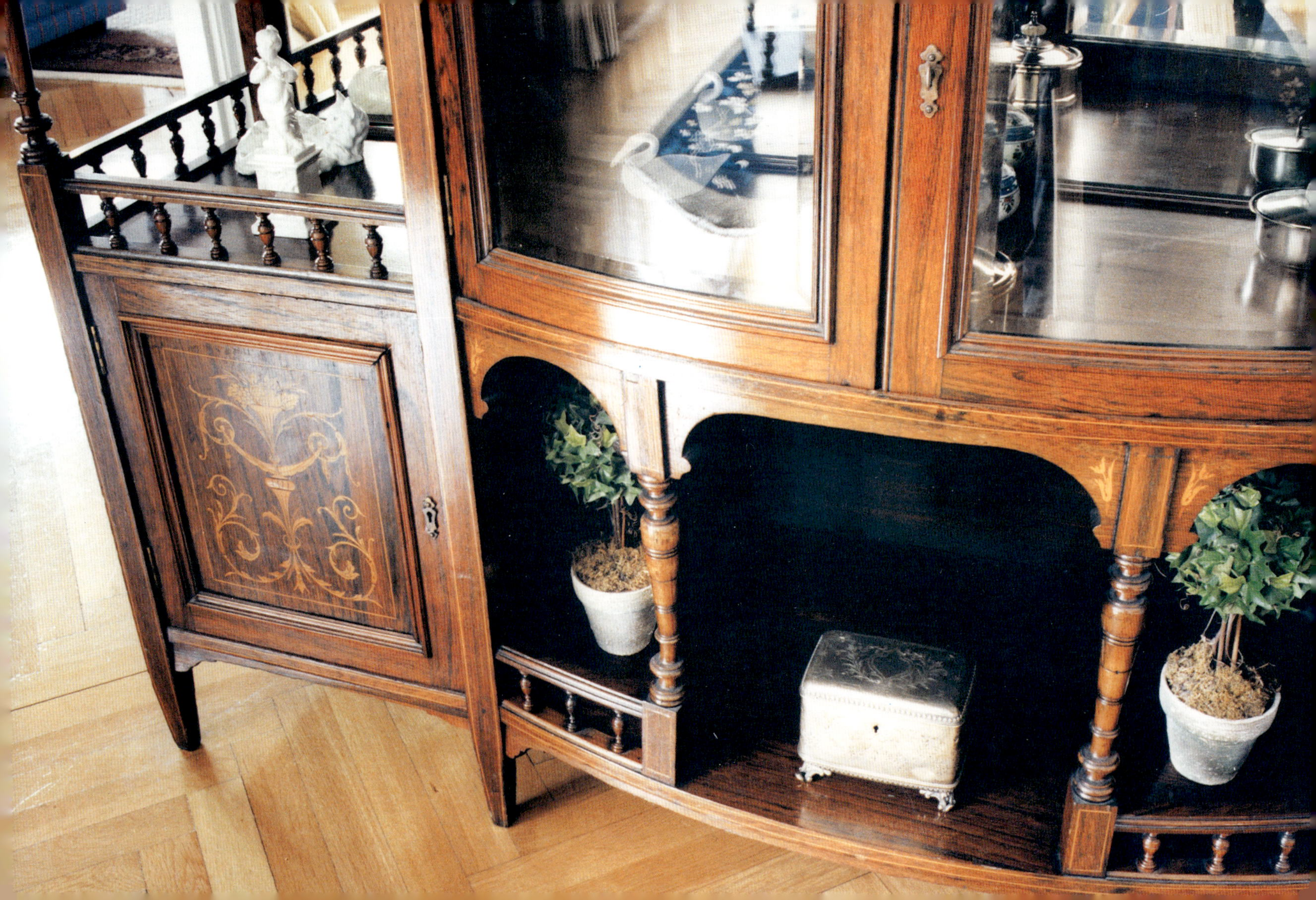

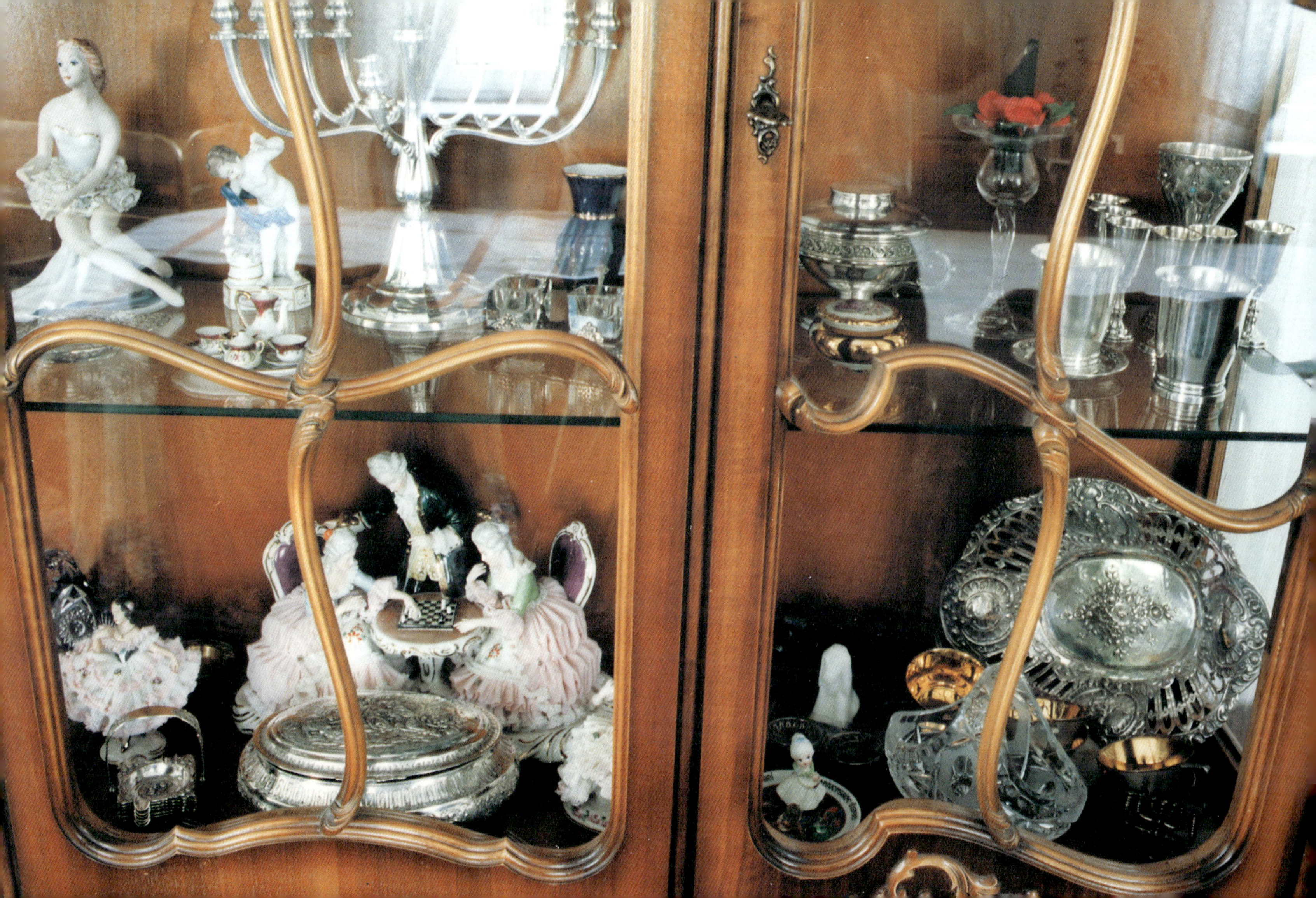

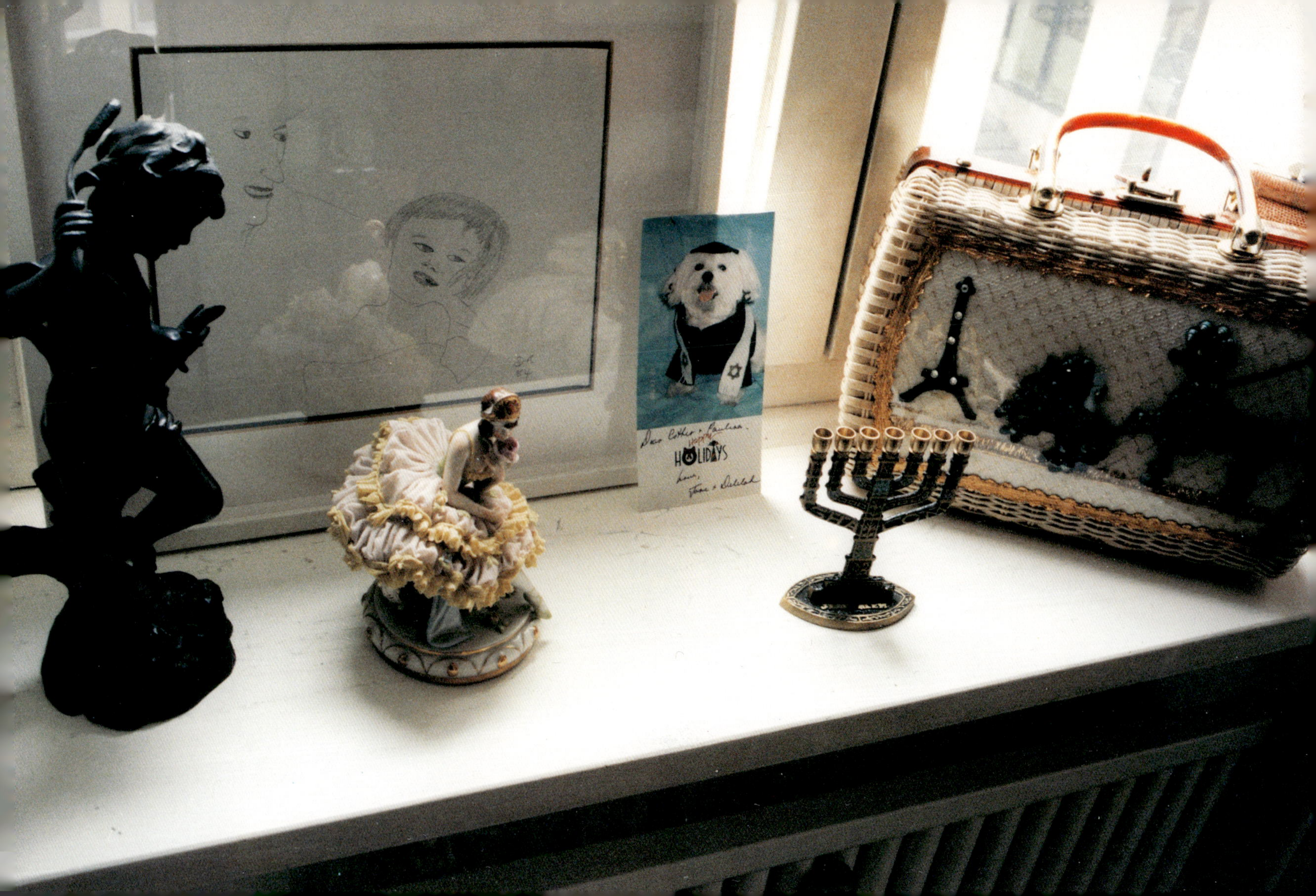
HOLIDAYS

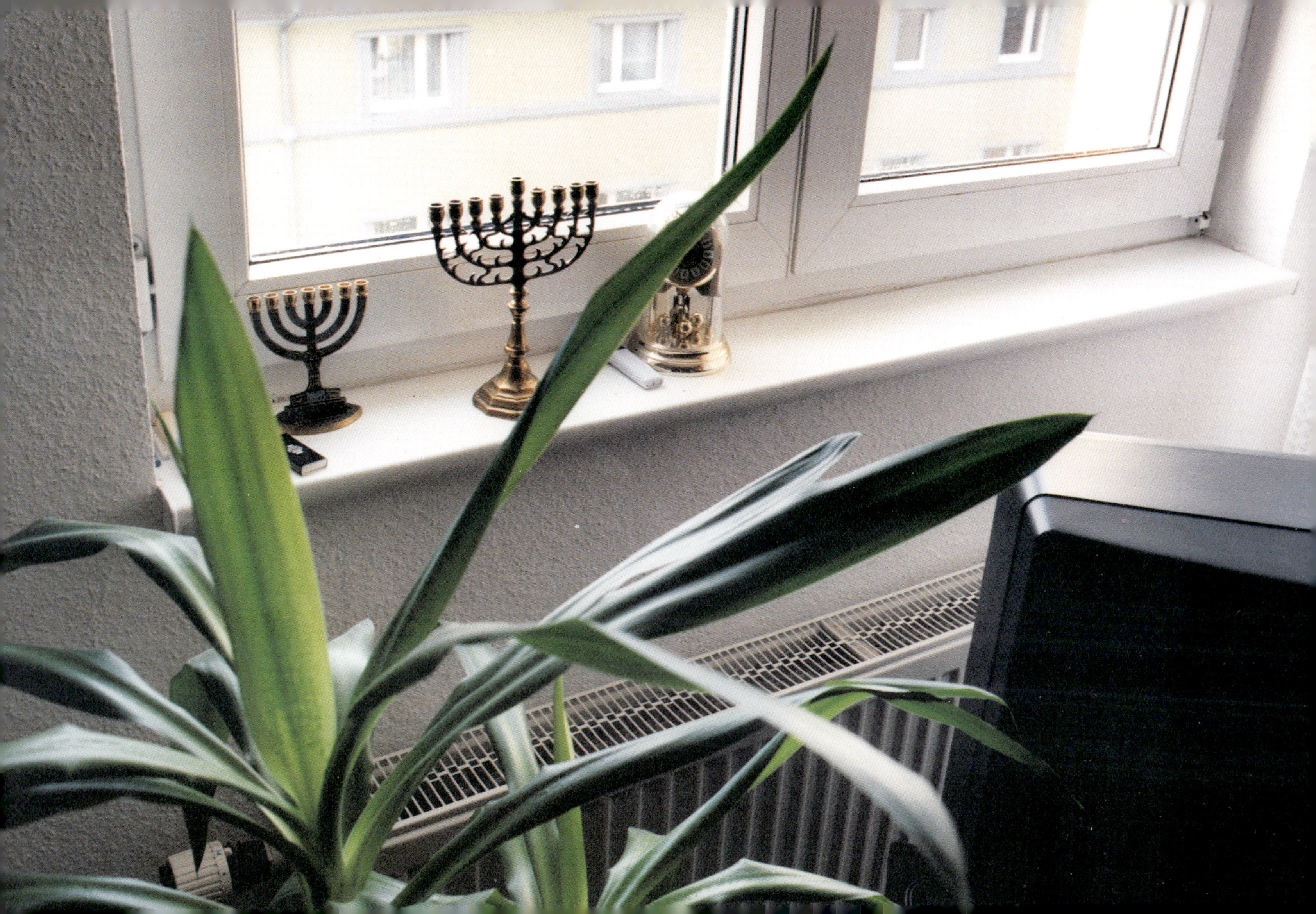

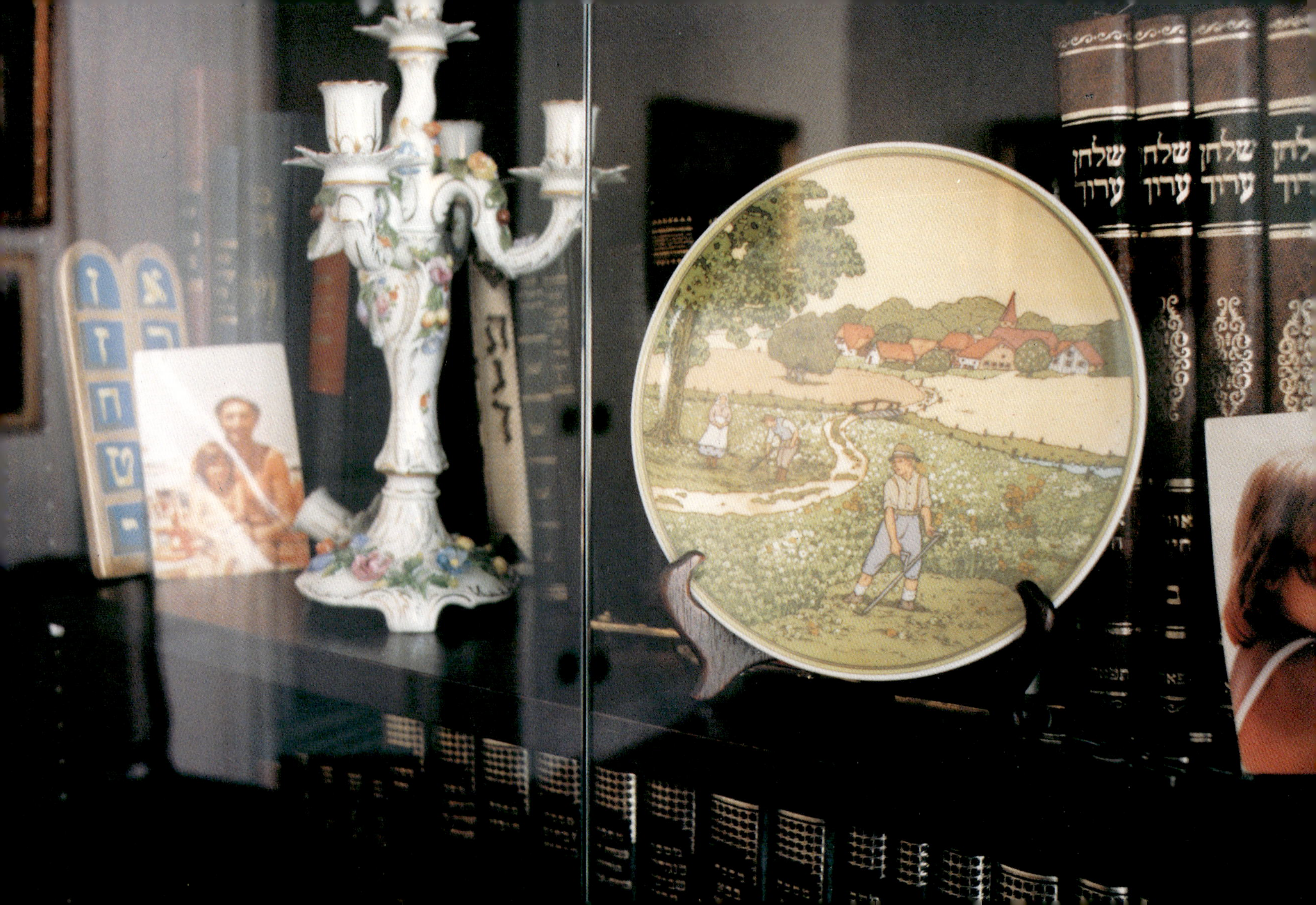

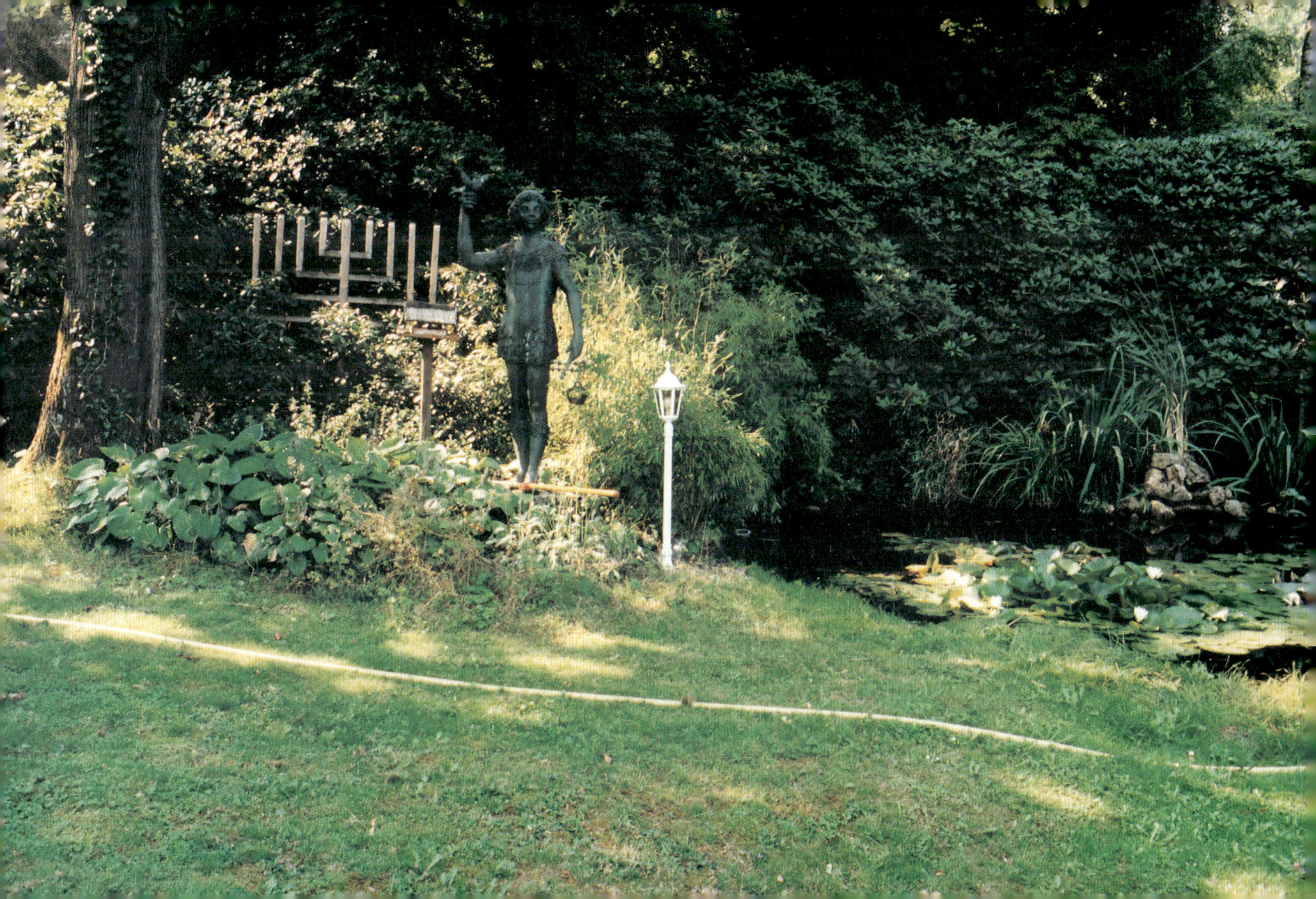

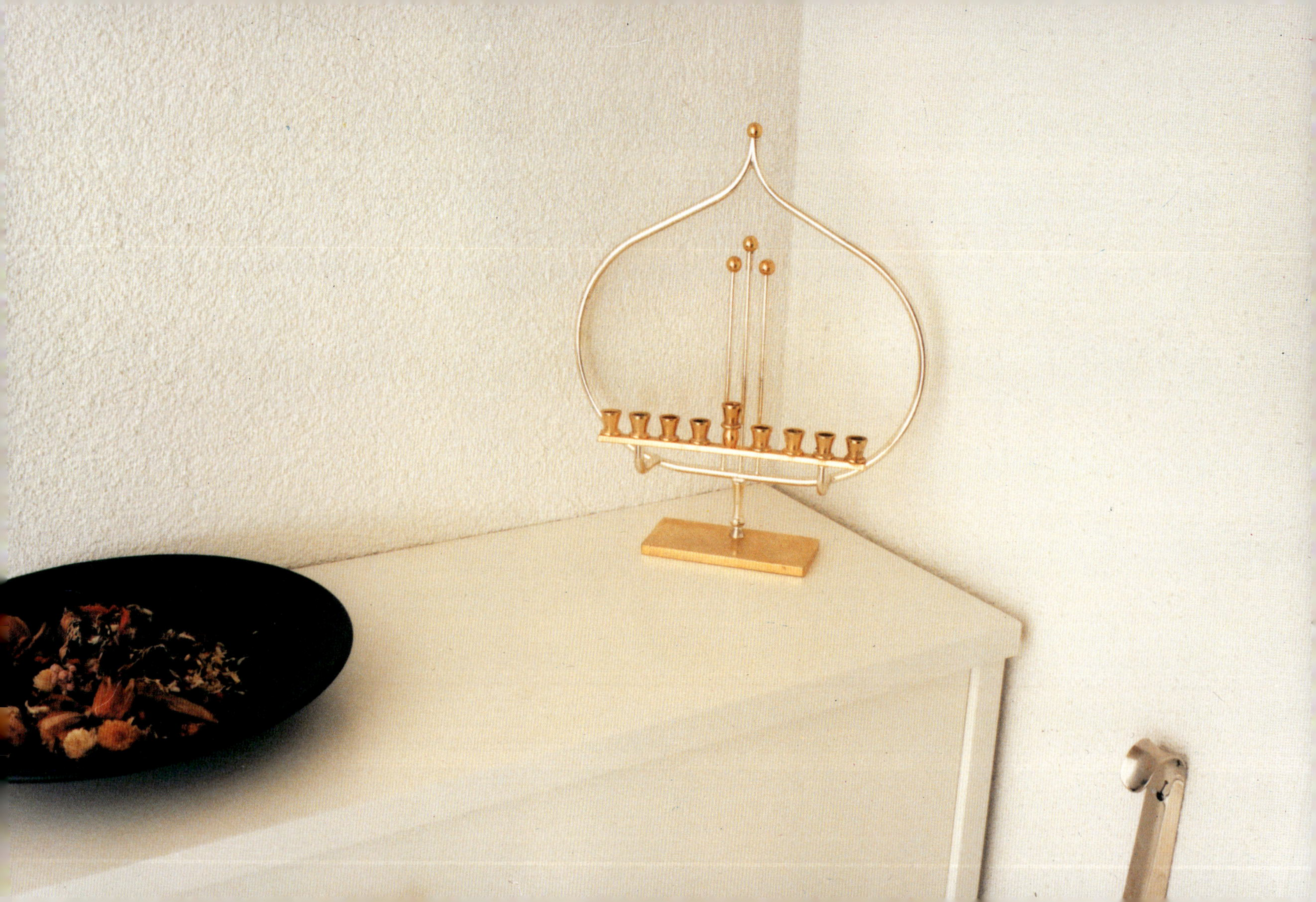

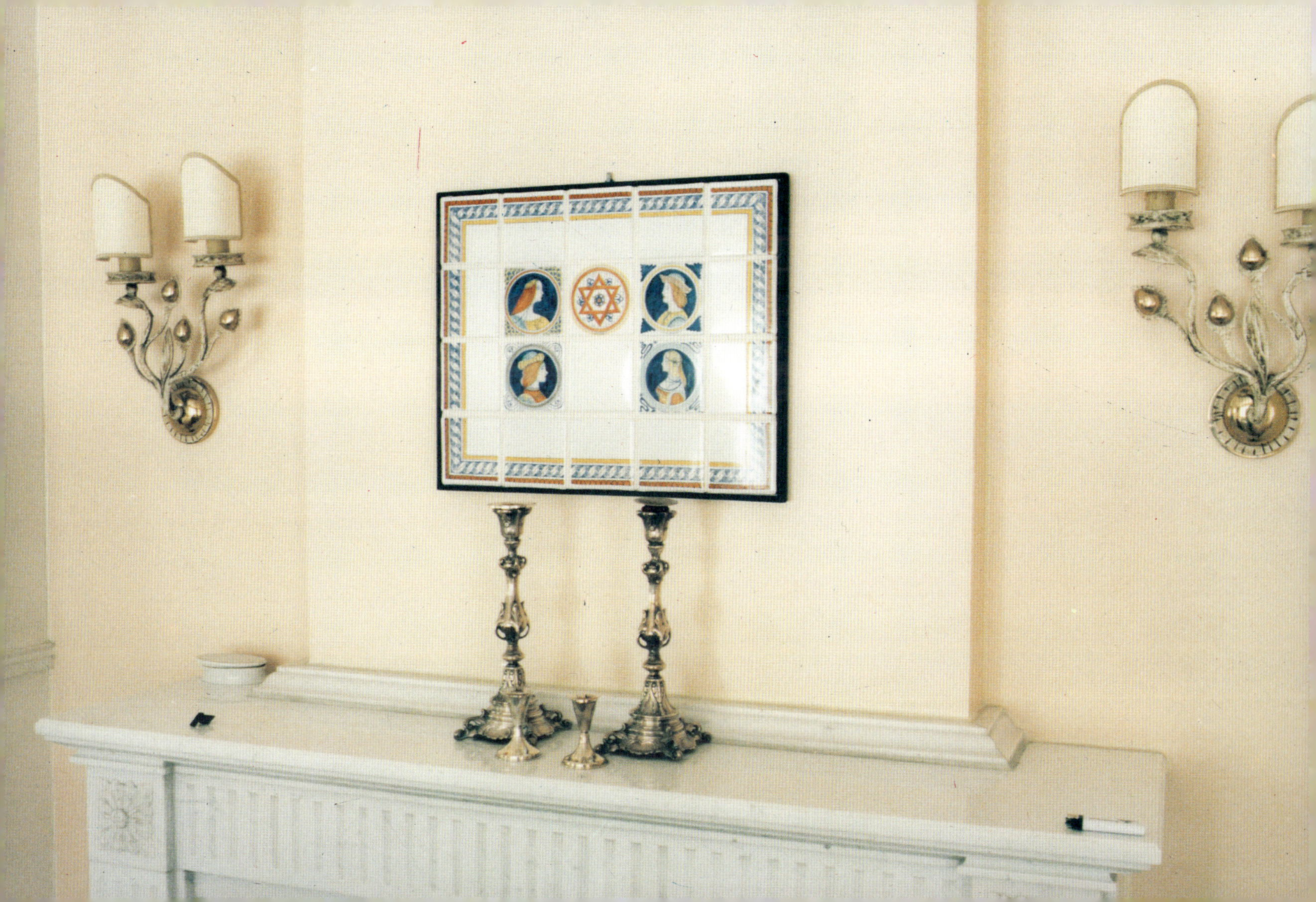

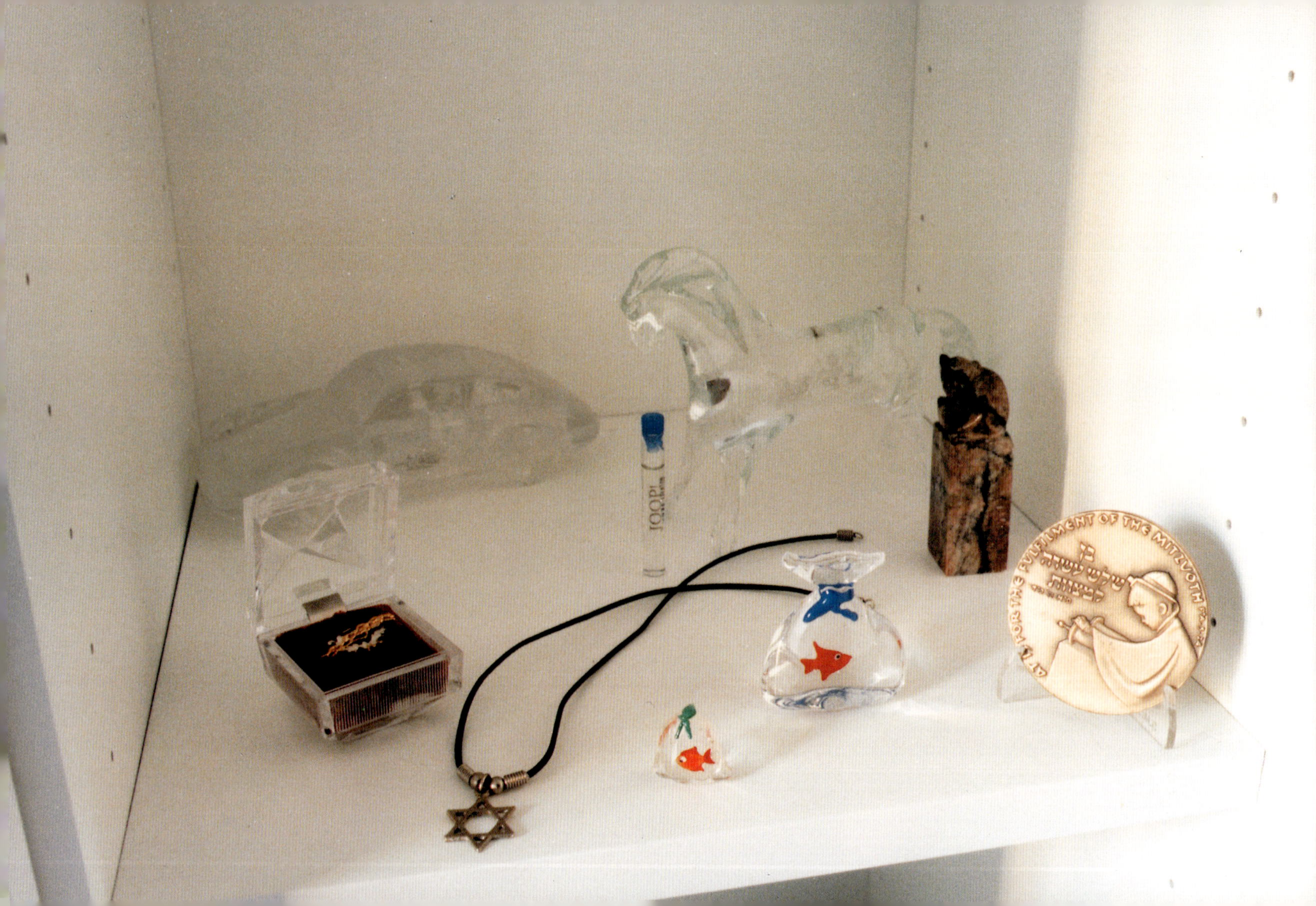
JOOP!
FULFILLMENT OF THE MITZVOTH

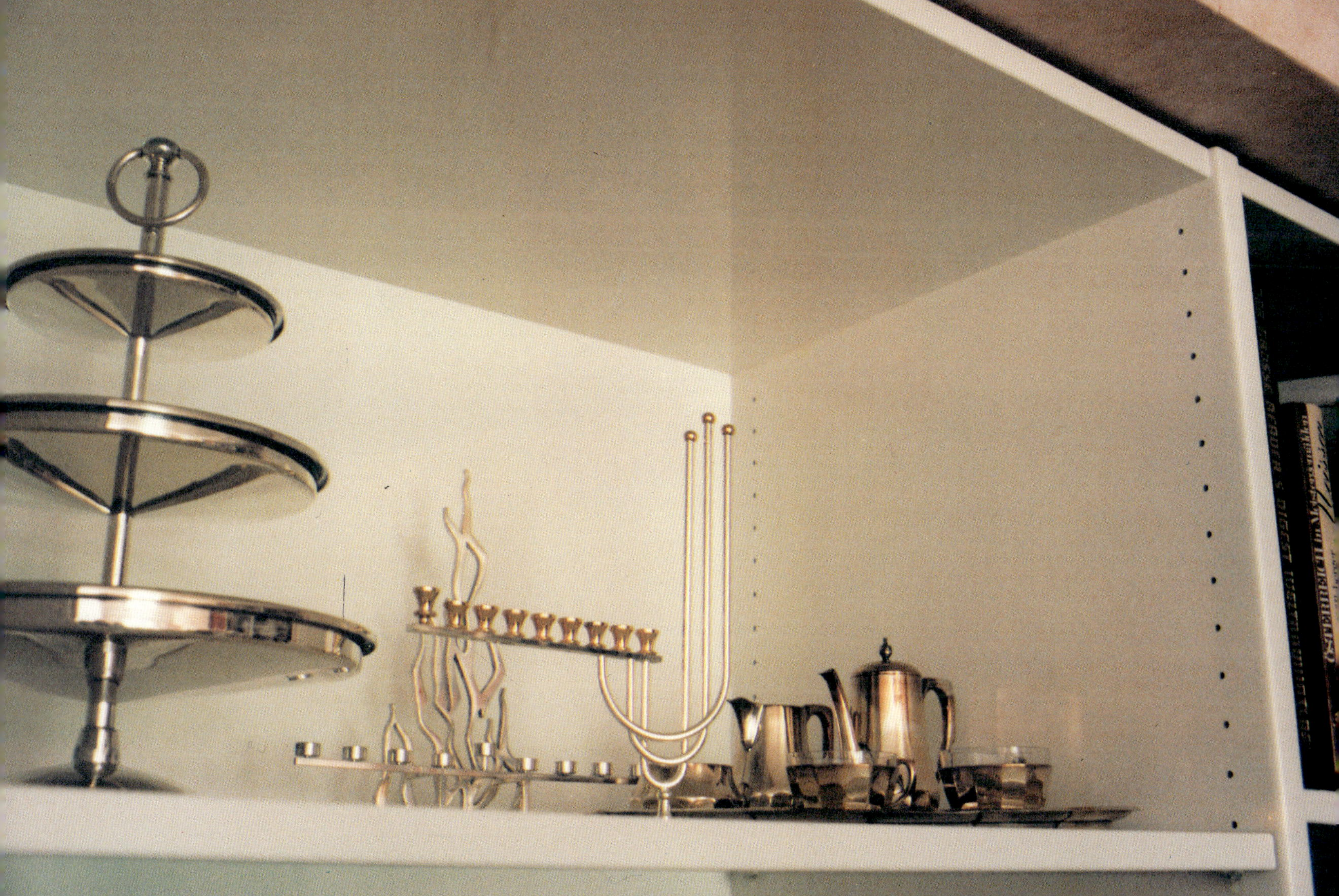

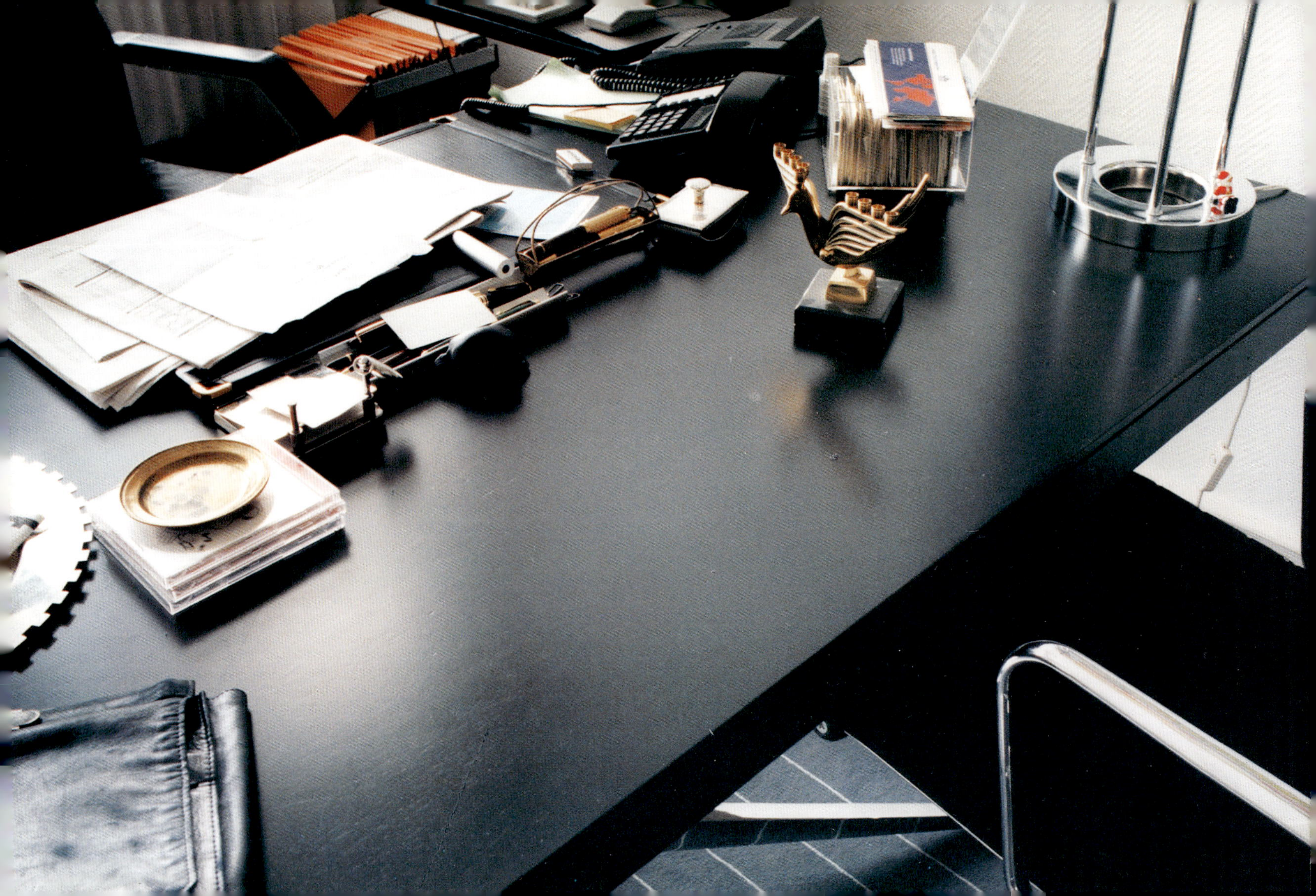

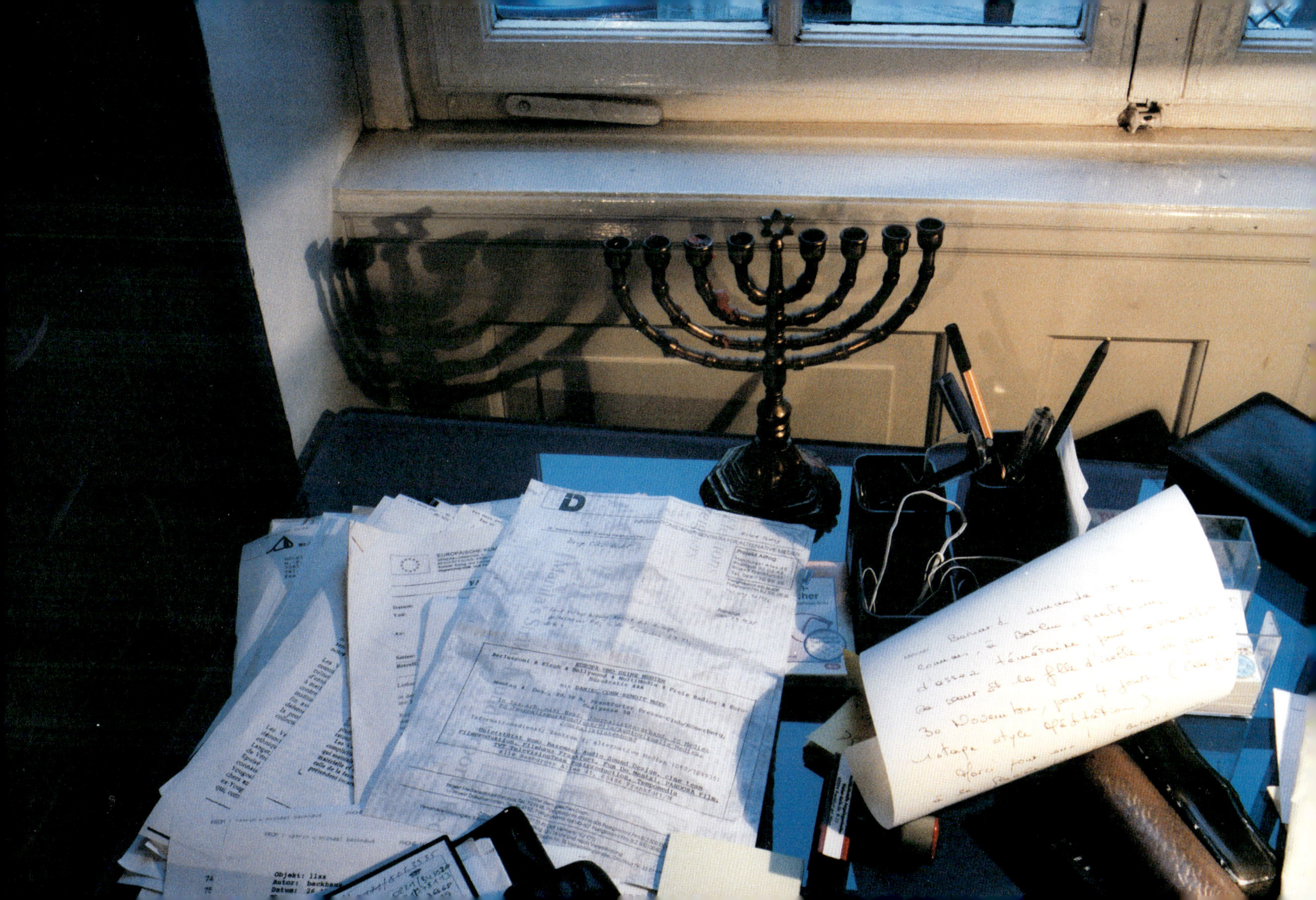

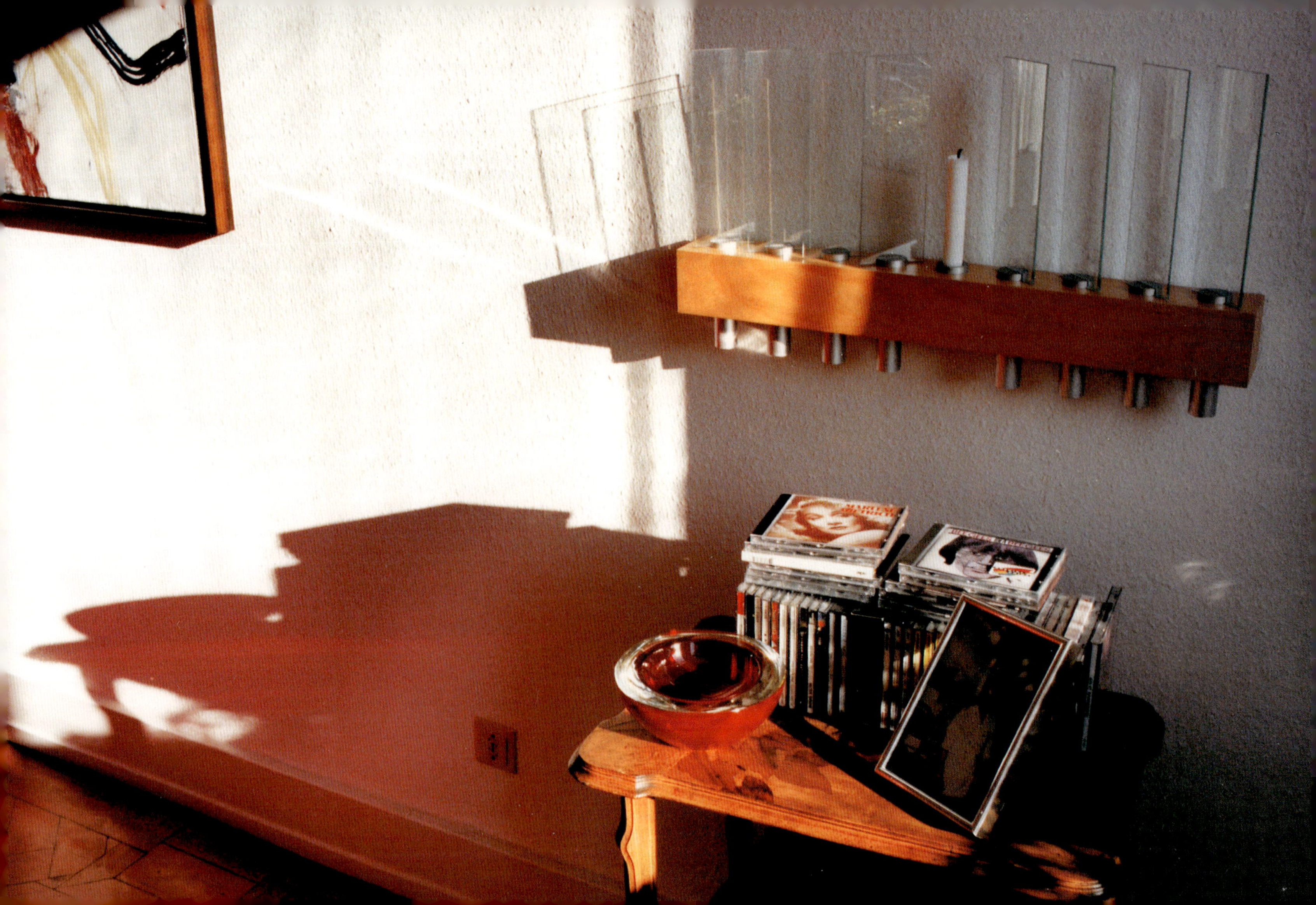

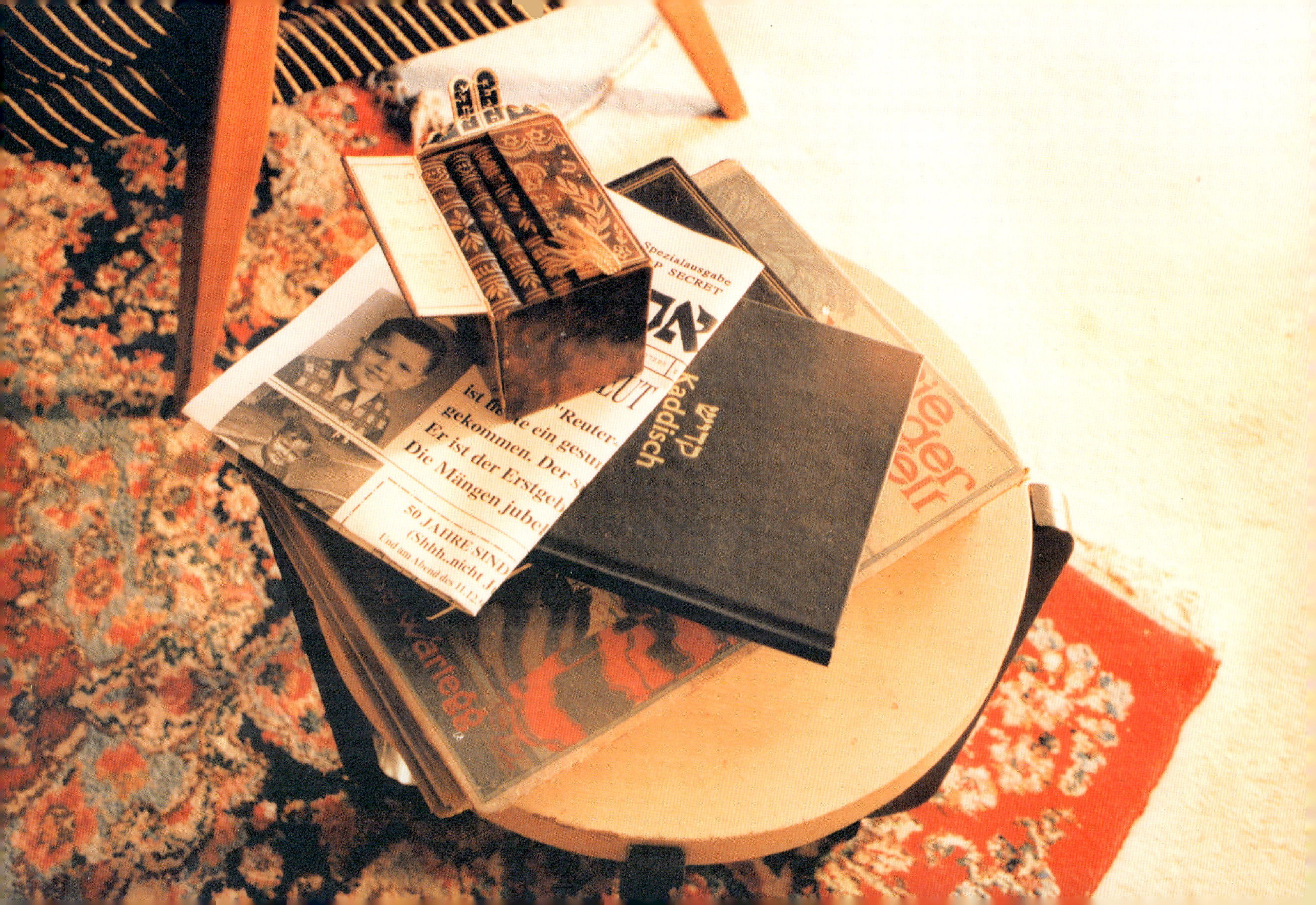
Spezialausgabe
TOP SECRET
kaddisch קדיש
ist heute ein gest
gekommen. Der s
Er ist der Erstgeb
Die Mängen jubel
50 JAHRE SIND
(Shhh...nicht J
Und am Abend des 11.12.

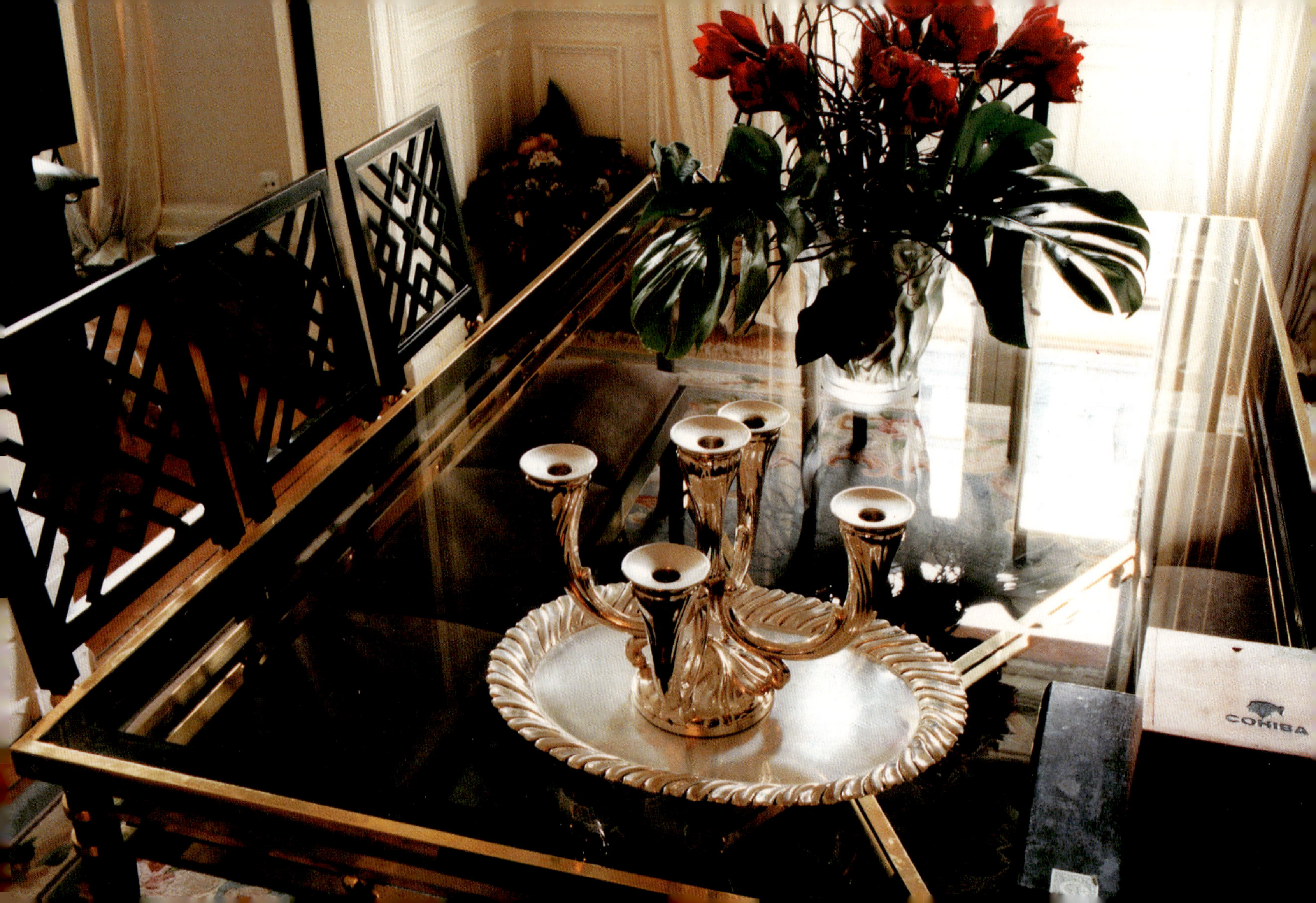

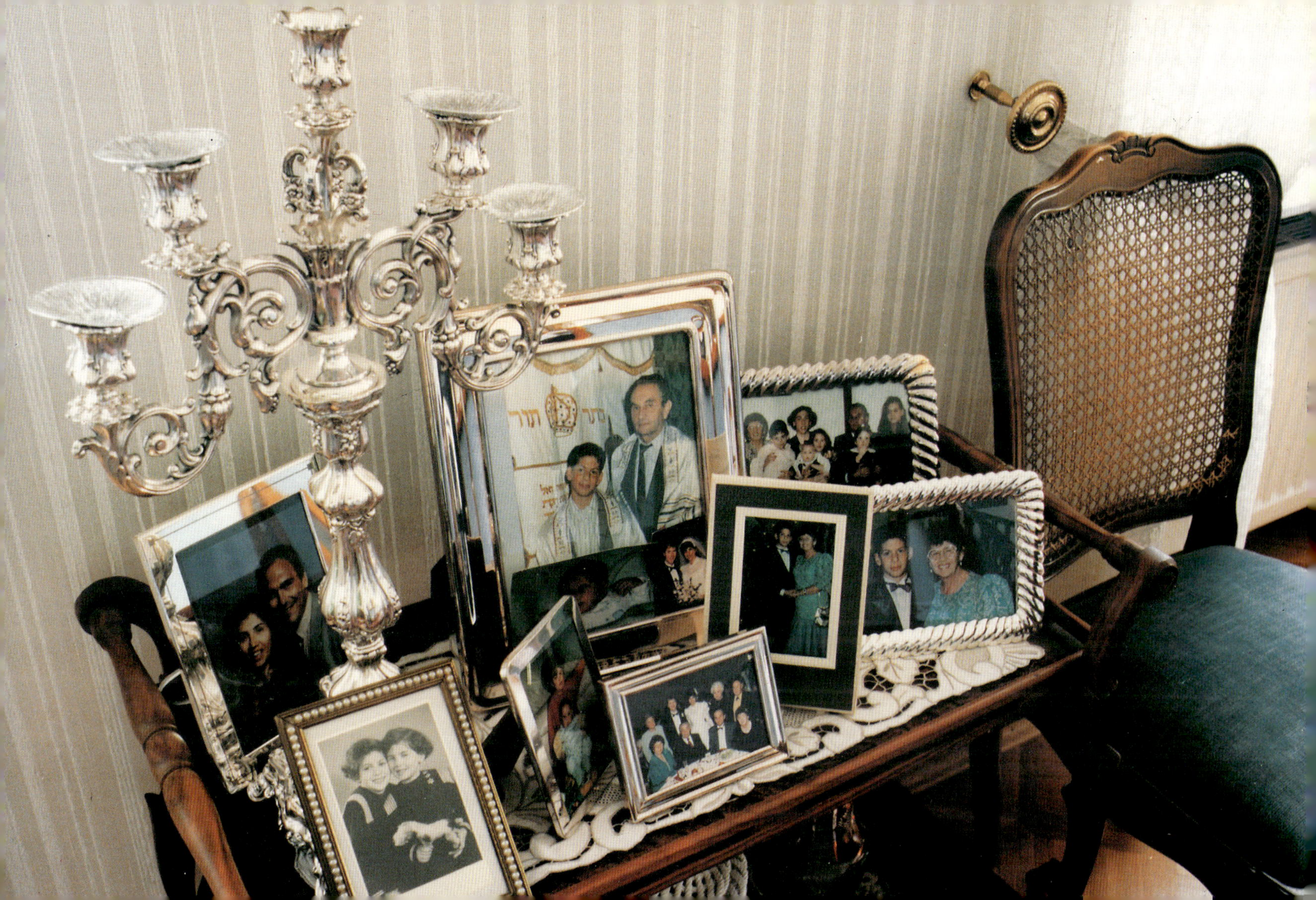

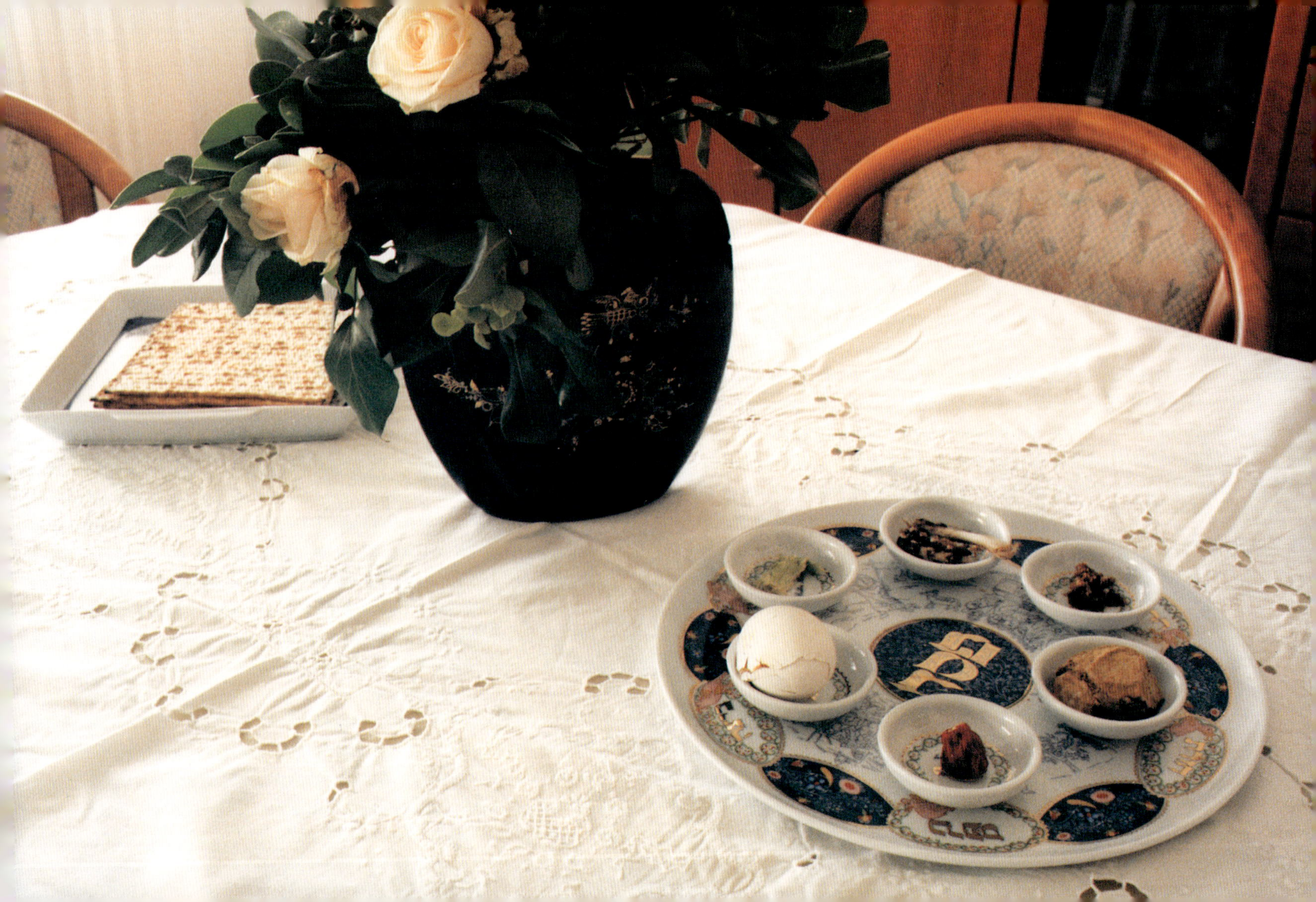

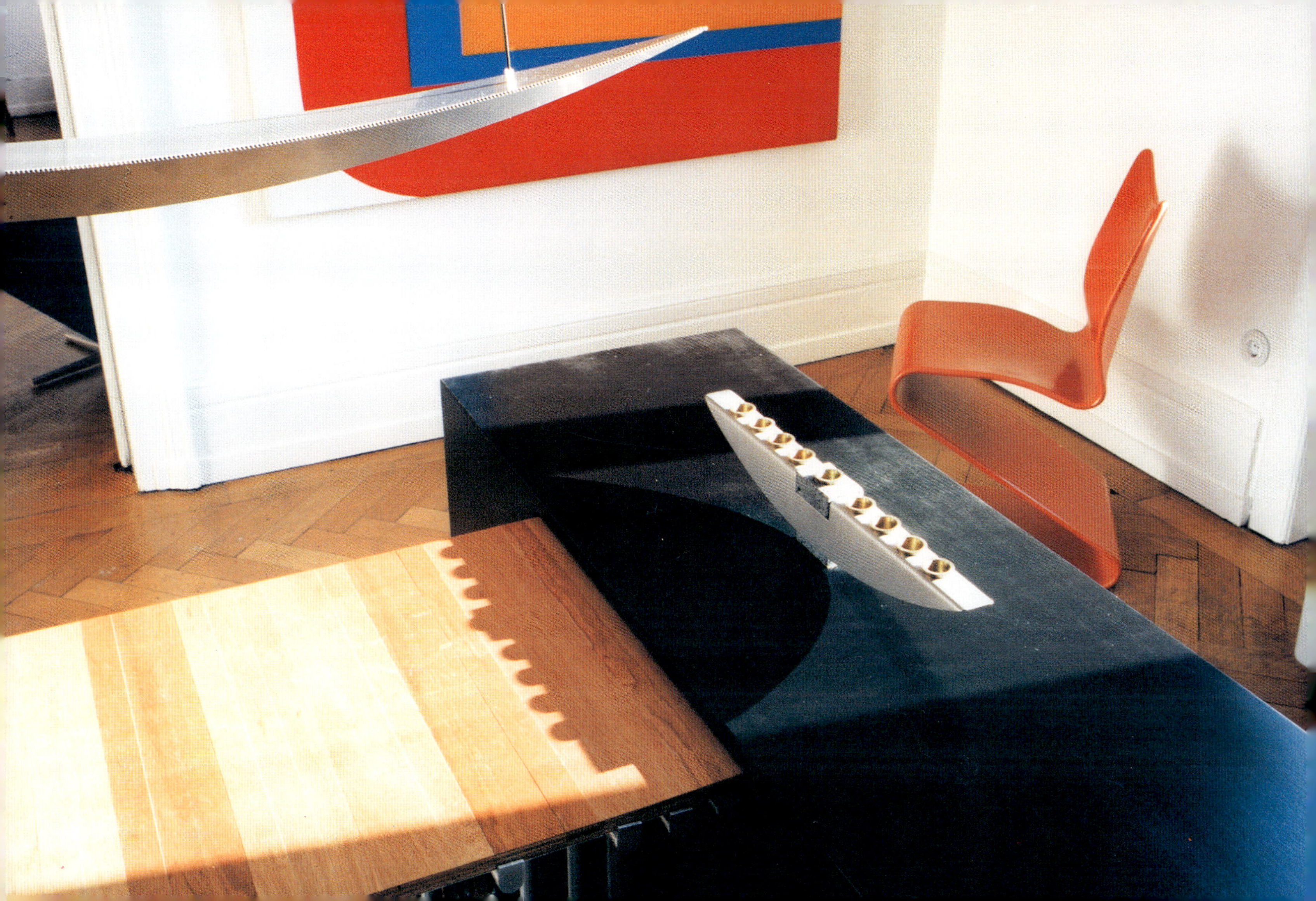

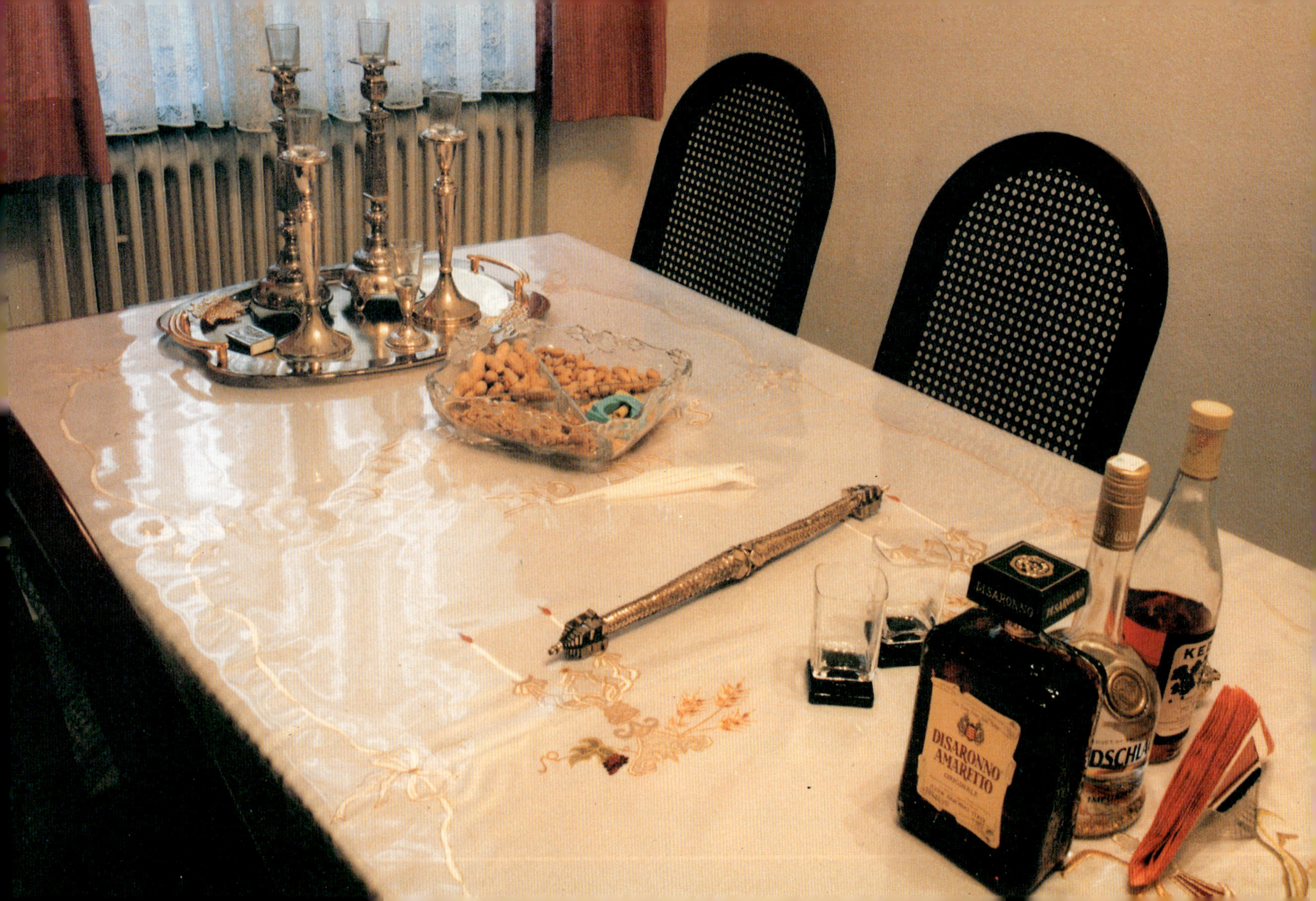

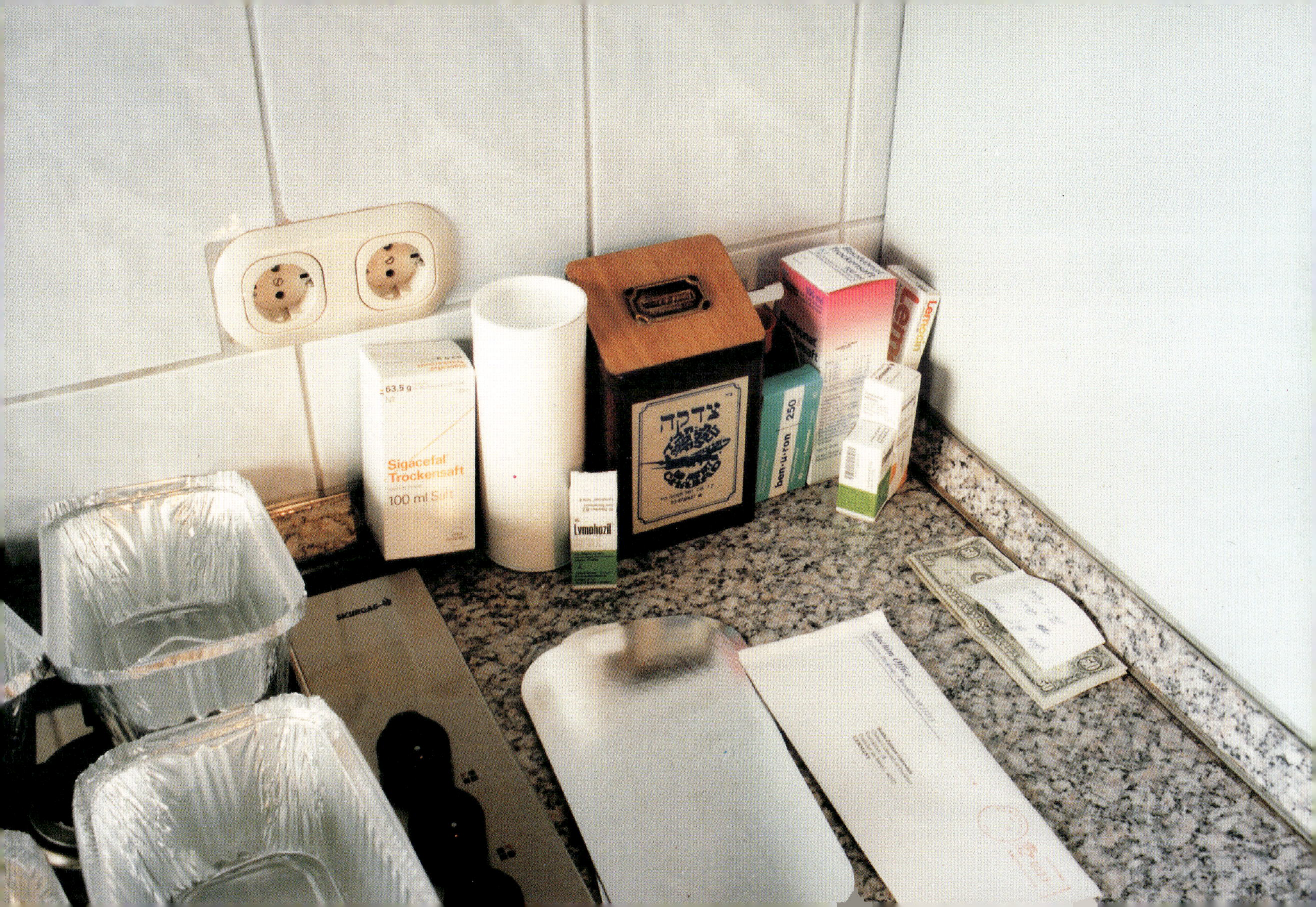

Sigacefal
Trockensaft
100 ml Saft
63,5 g
Lvmohazil
צדקה
ben-u-ron 250
Lemon
SICURGAS

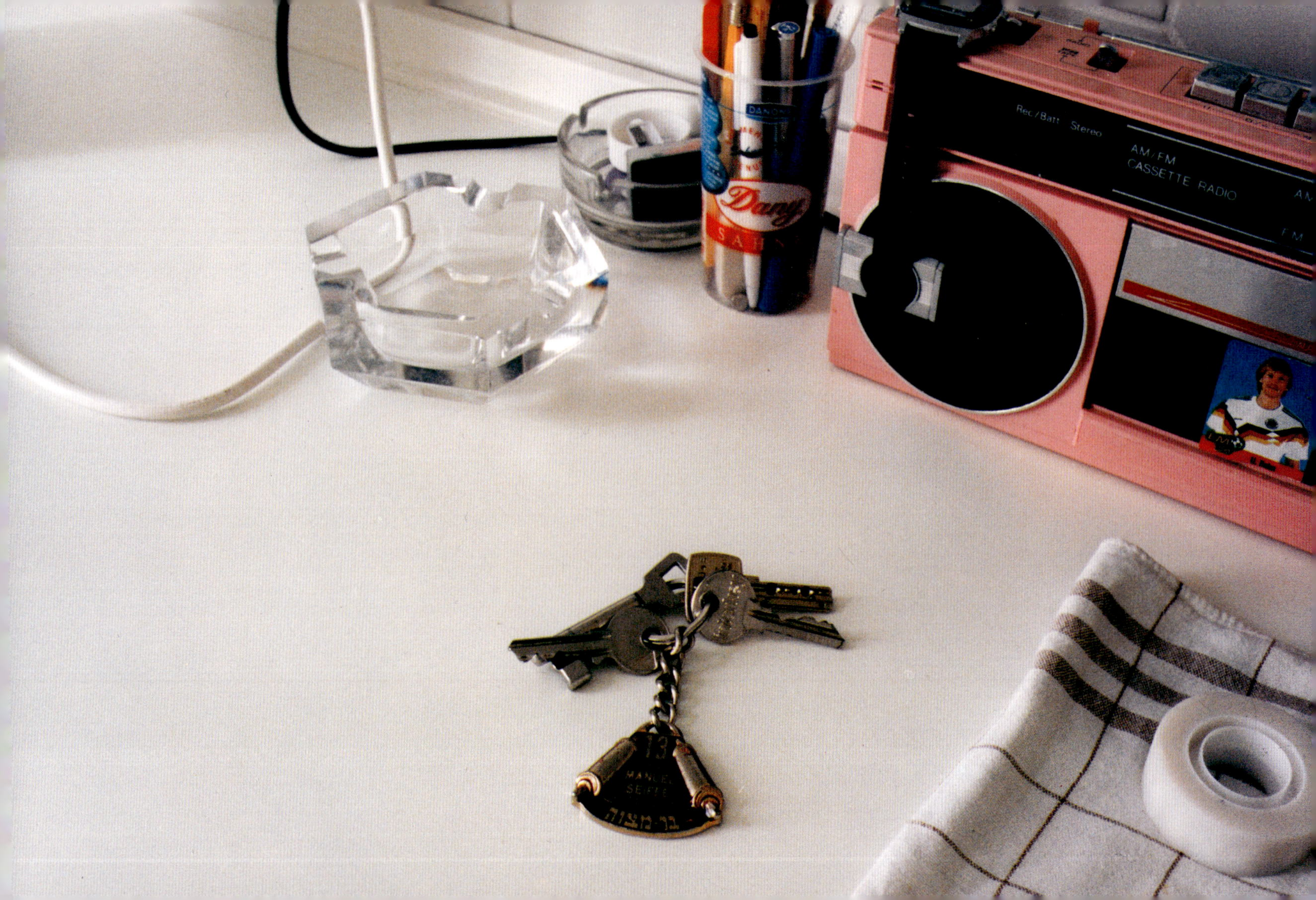

Rec/Batt Stereo
AM/FM
CASSETTE RADIO
Dany
13

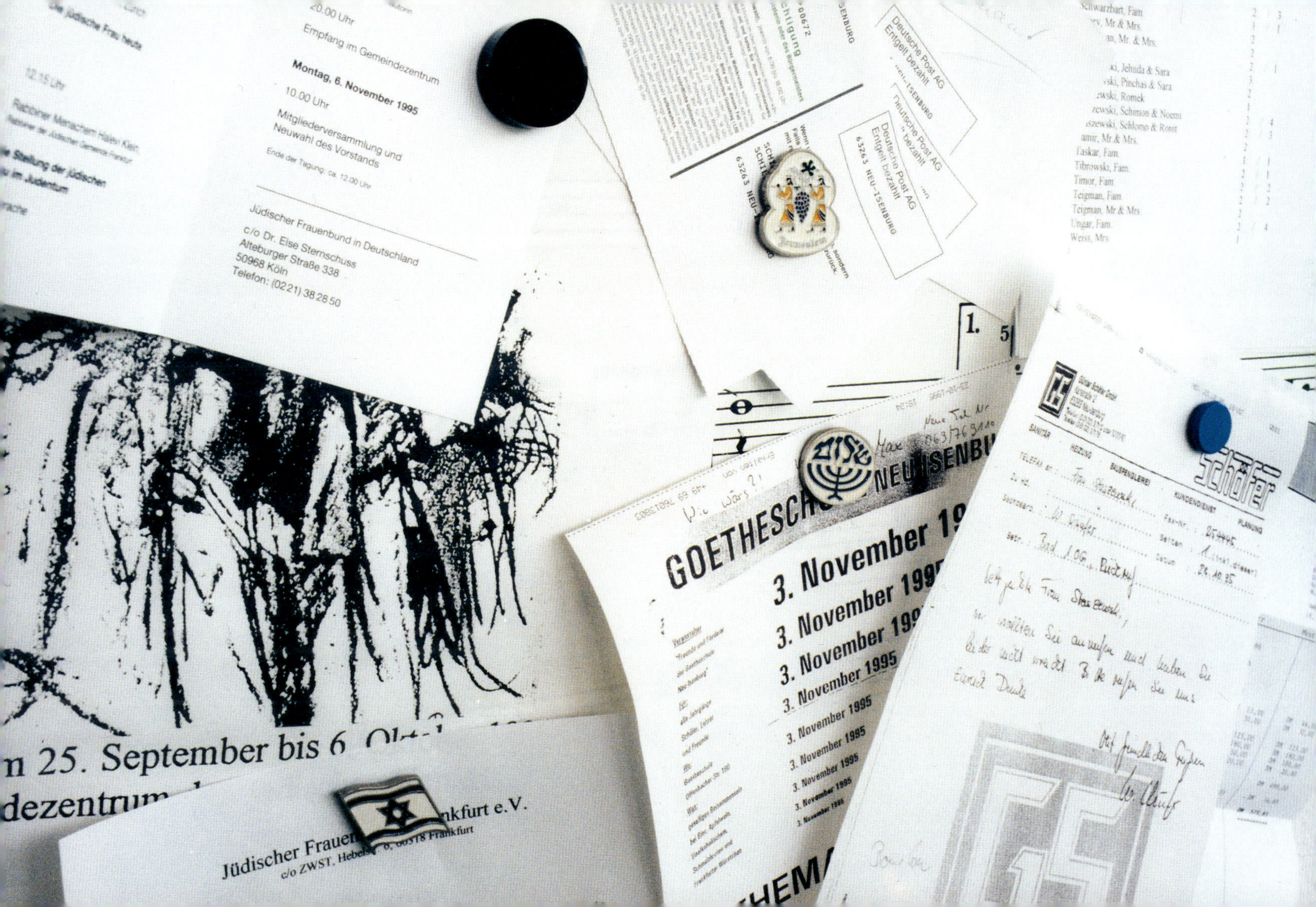
20.00 Uhr
Empfang im Gemeindezentrum

Montag, 6. November 1995
10.00 Uhr
Mitgliederversammlung und
Neuwahl des Vorstands
Ende der Tagung: ca. 12.00 Uhr

Jüdischer Frauenbund in Deutschland
c/o Dr. Else Sternschuss
Alteburger Straße 338
50968 Köln
Telefon: (02 21) 38 28 50

Schwarzbart, Fam
..rev, Mr & Mrs
..an, Mr. & Mrs.
..ki, Jehuda & Sara
..vski, Pinchas & Sara
..zwski, Romek
..zewski, Schimon & Noemi
..aszewski, Schlomo & Roni
..amir, Mr & Mrs.
..askar, Fam.
..browski, Fam.
Timor, Fam
Teigman, Fam
Teigman, Mr & Mrs
Ungar, Fam.
Weiss, Mrs

Deutsche Post AG
Entgelt bezahlt
SCH...
63263 NEU-ISENBURG

Deutsche Post AG
Entgelt bezahlt
63263 NEU-ISENBURG

GOETHESCHULE NEU-ISENBURG
3. November 1995
3. November 1995
3. November 1995
3. November 1995
3. November 1995
3. November 1995
3. November 1995
3. November 1995
3. November 1995
3. November 1995

Veranstalter
"Freunde und Förderer
der Goetheschule
Neu-Isenburg"
für
alle Jahrgänge
Schüler, Lehrer
und Freunde
Ort:
Goetheschule
Offenbacher Str. 160

Schöfer
SANITÄR   HEIZUNG   BAUSPENGLEREI   KUNDENDIENST   PLANUNG
TELEFAX an:

n 25. September bis 6. Oktober

Jüdischer Frauen... Frankfurt e.V.
c/o ZWST, Hebelstr. 6, 60318 Frankfurt

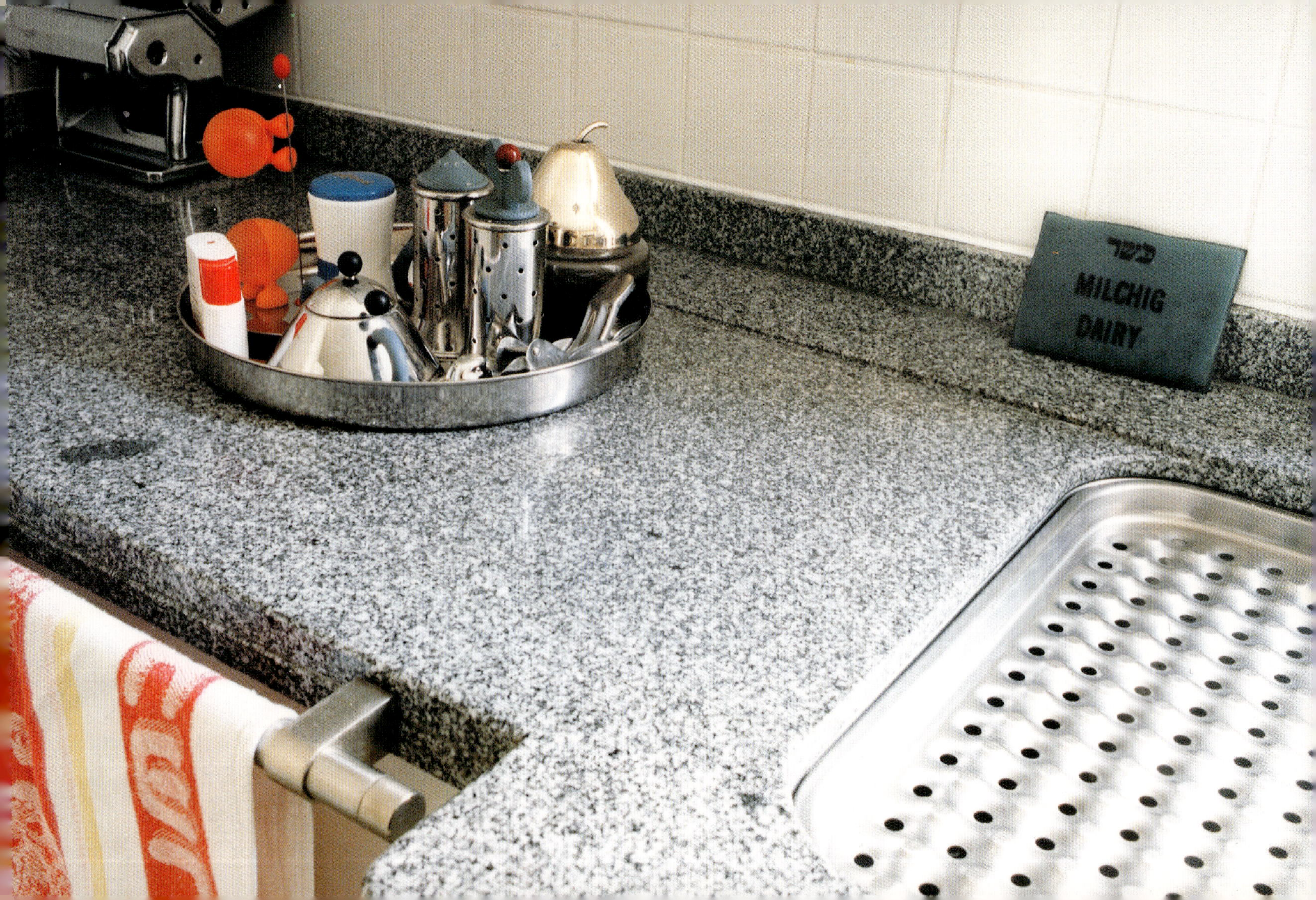
בשׂר
MILCHIG
DAIRY

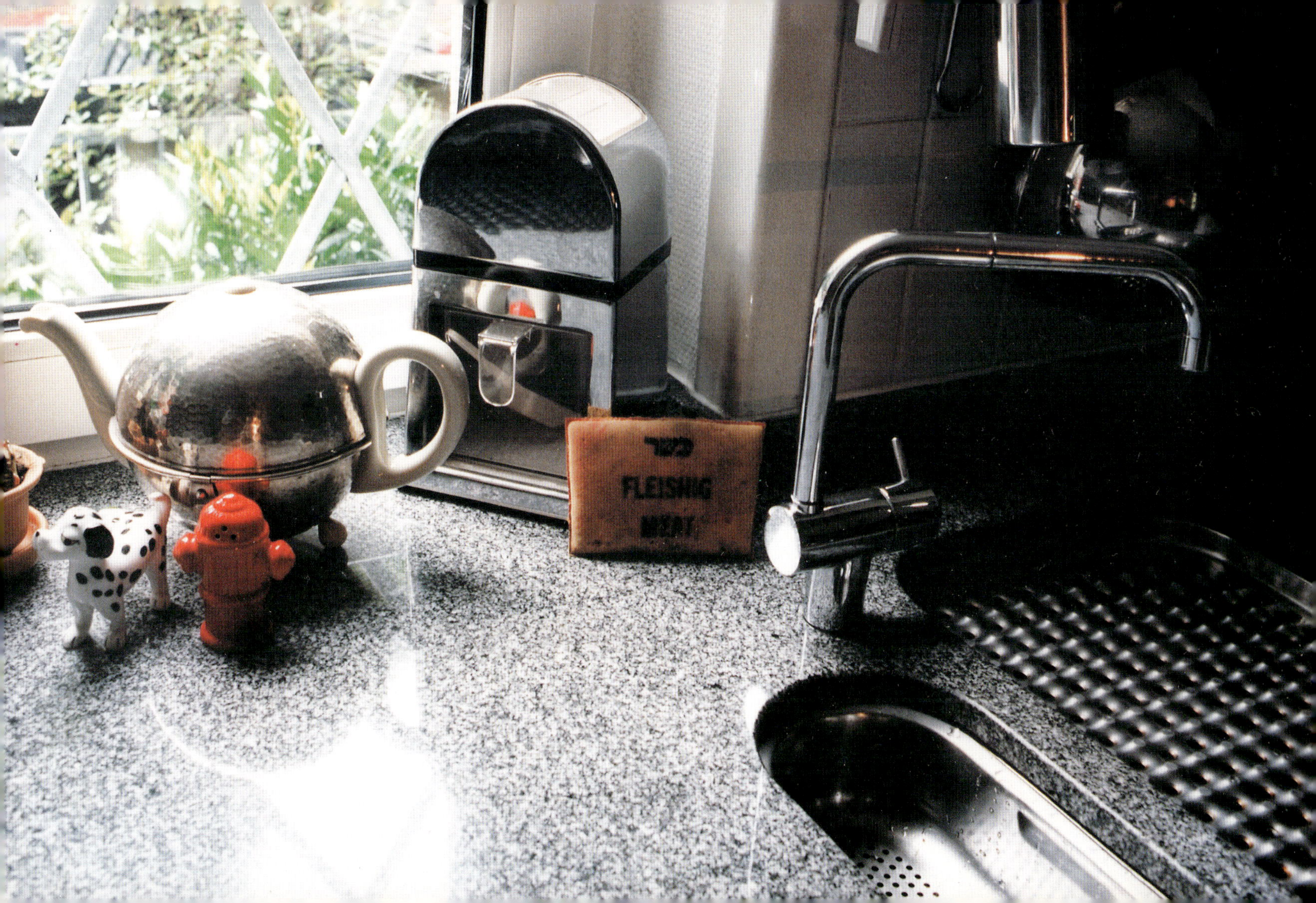

בשרי
FLEISHIG
MEAT

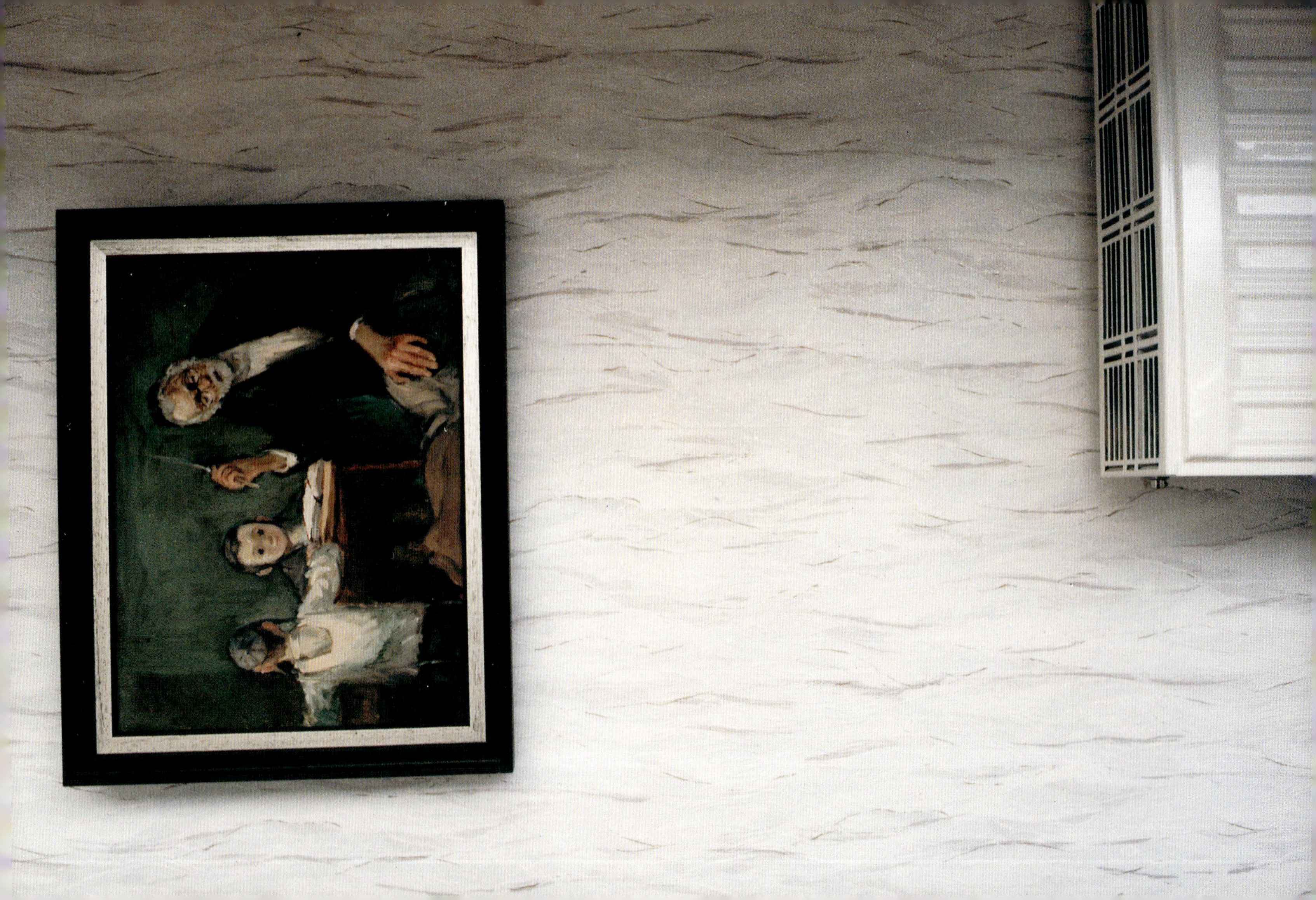

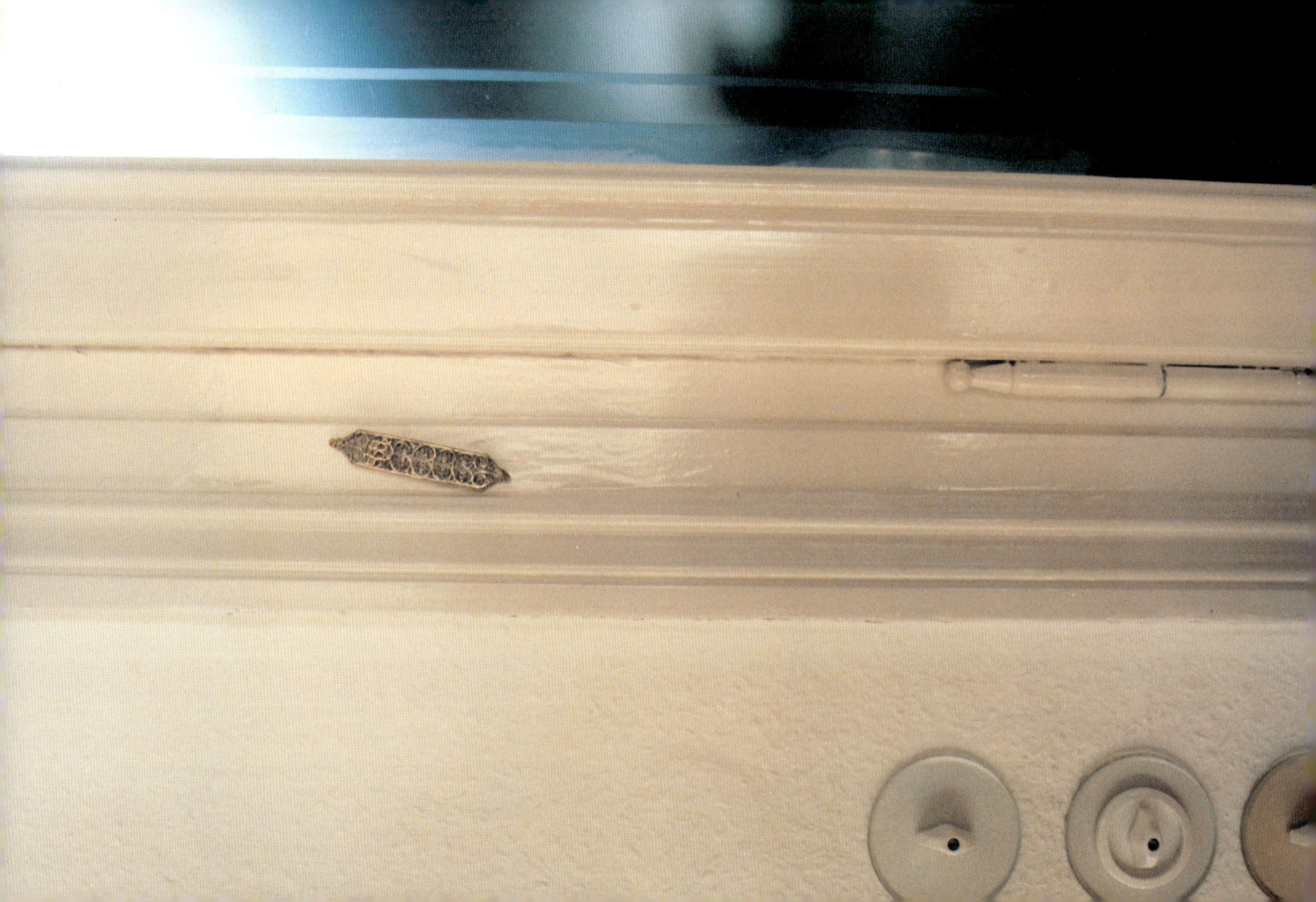

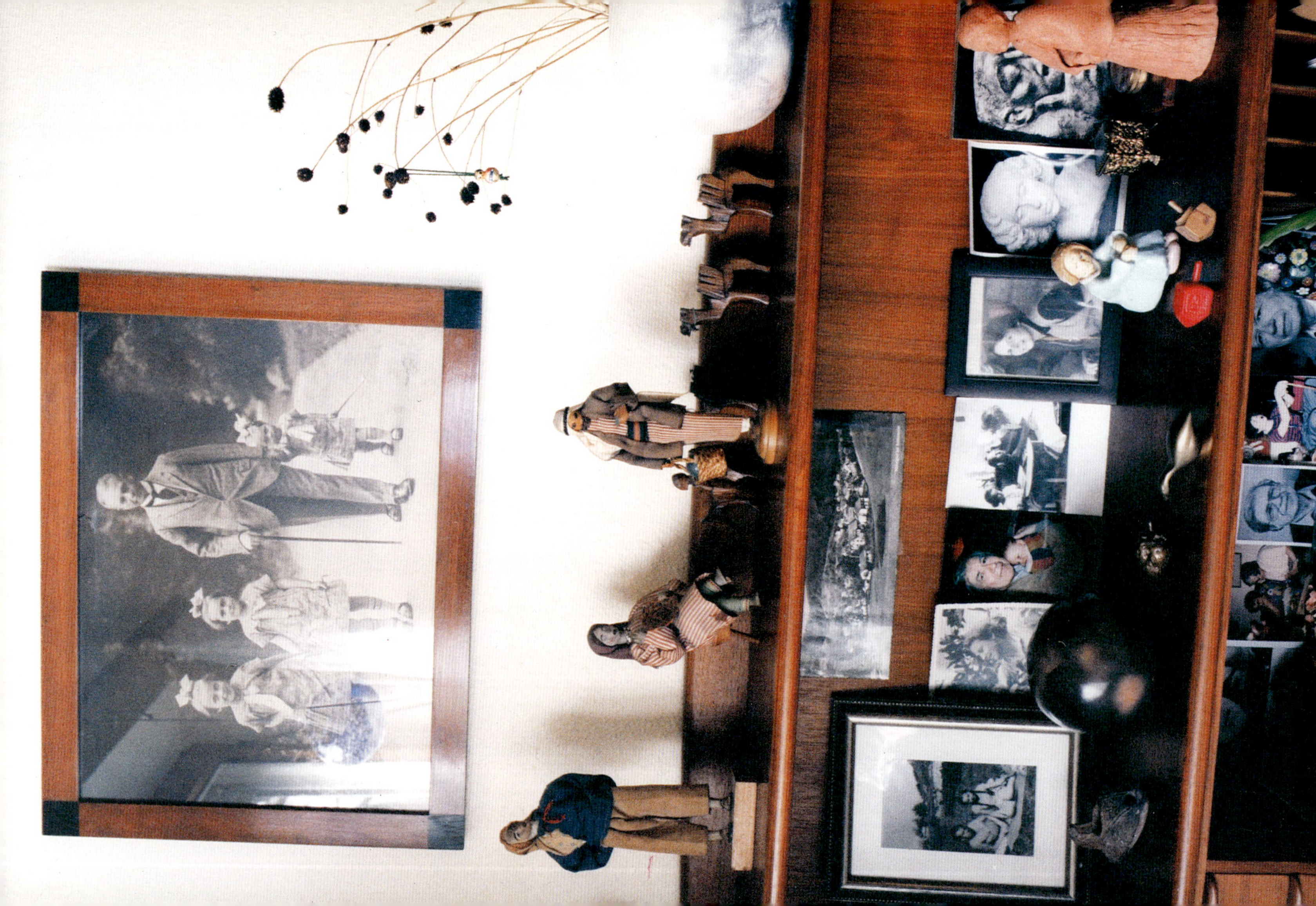

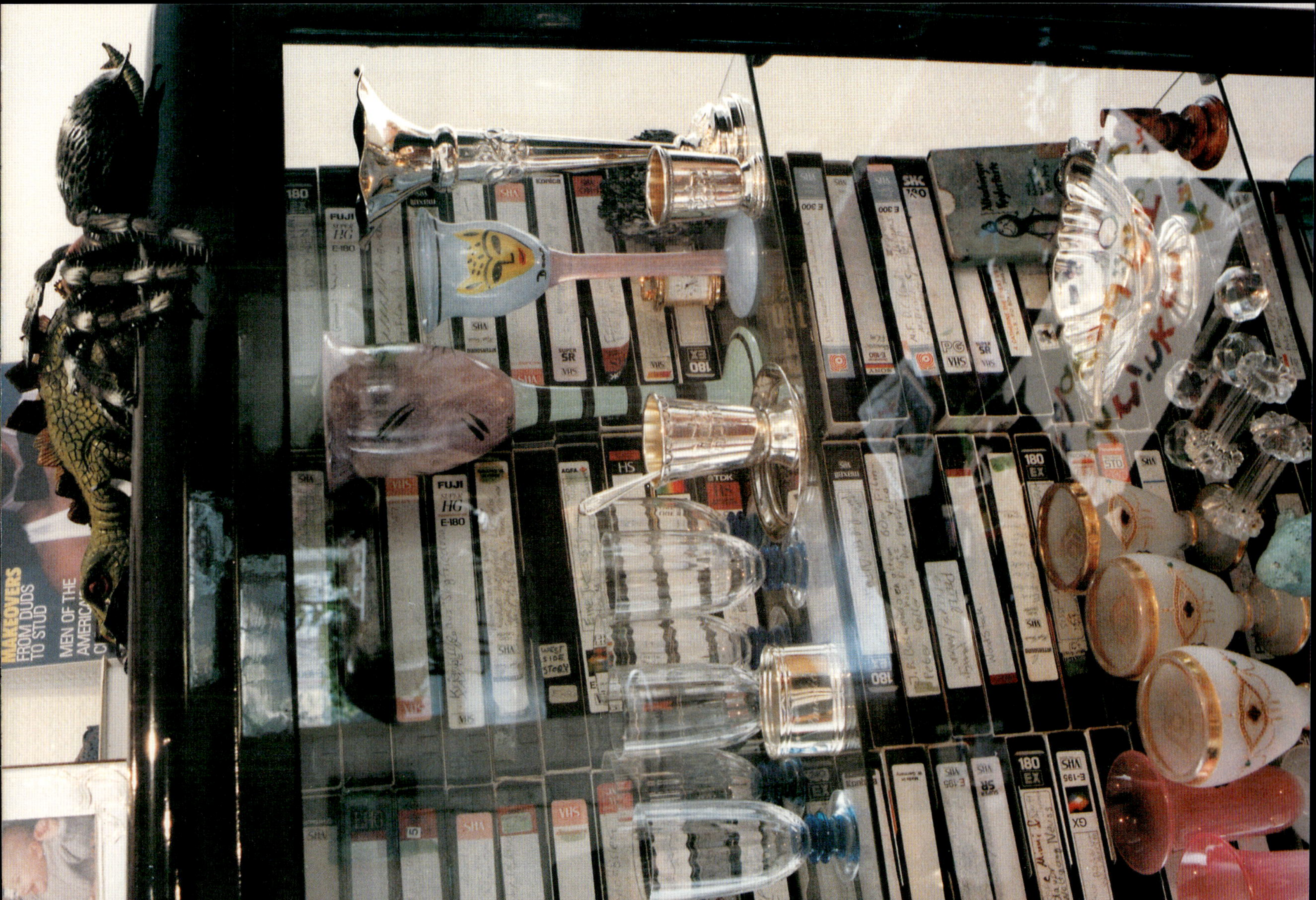

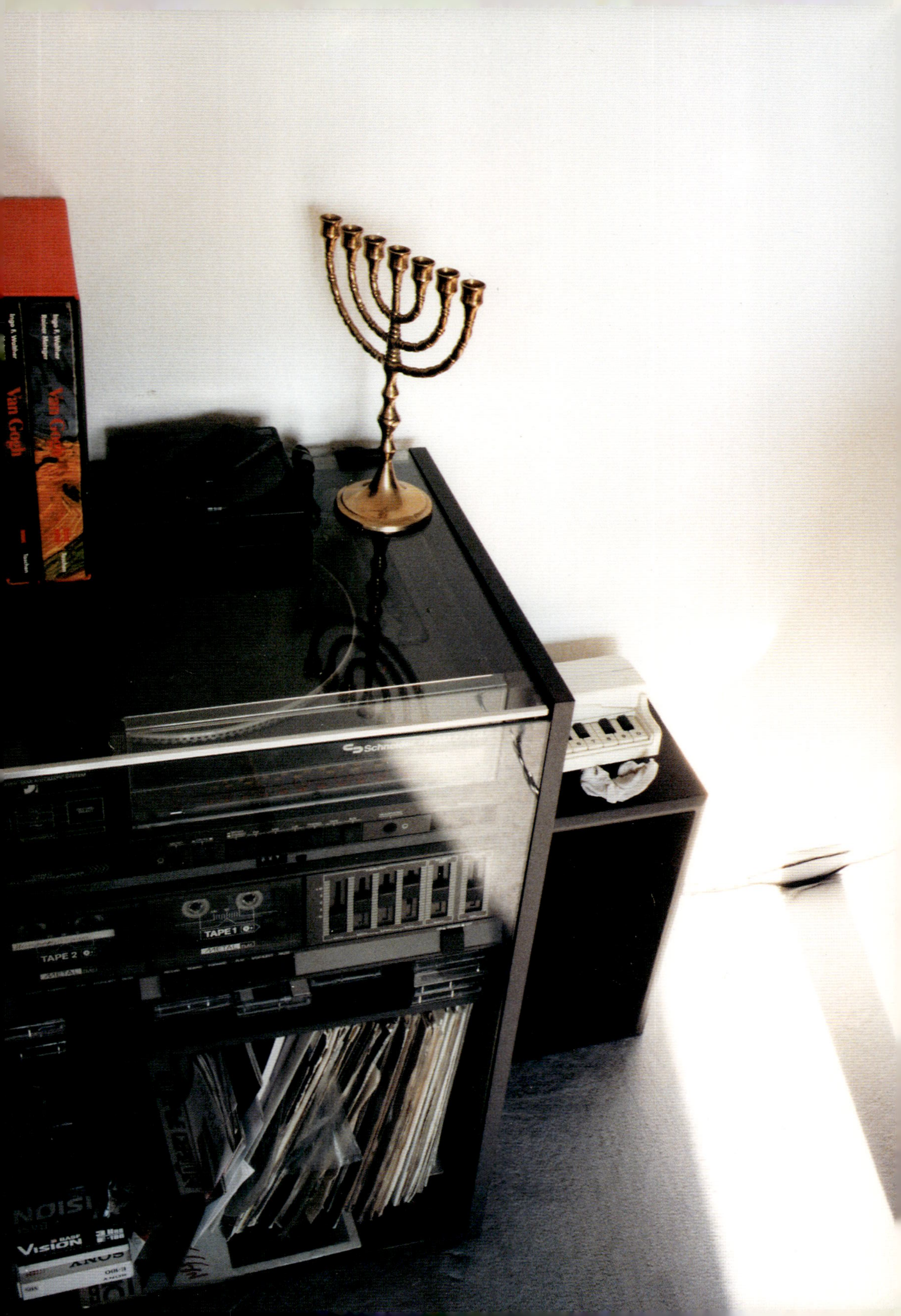

Ingo F. Walther
Rainer Metzger
Van Gogh
Taschen
Van Gogh
TAPE 1
TAPE 2
Schneider
Vision
SONY

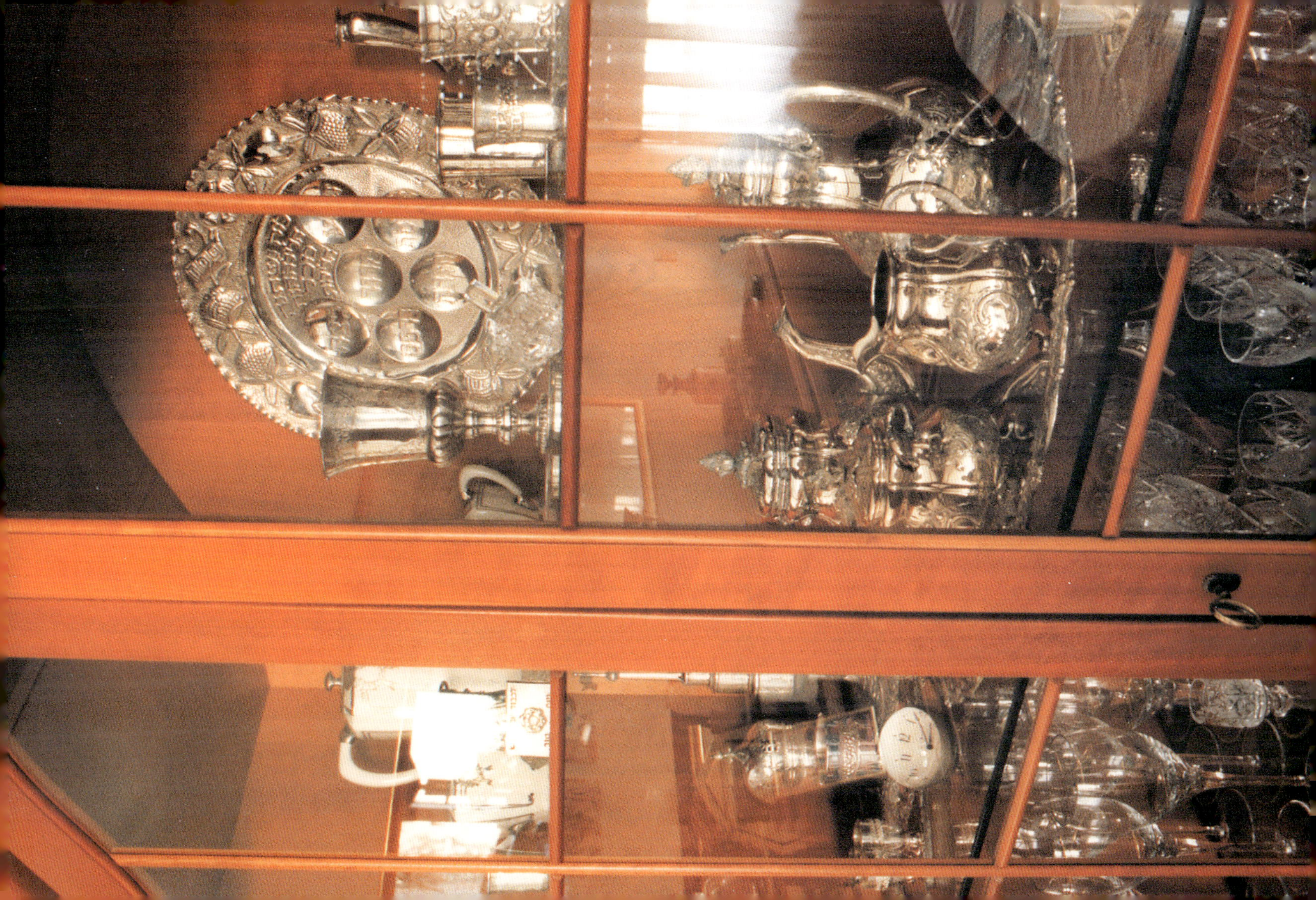

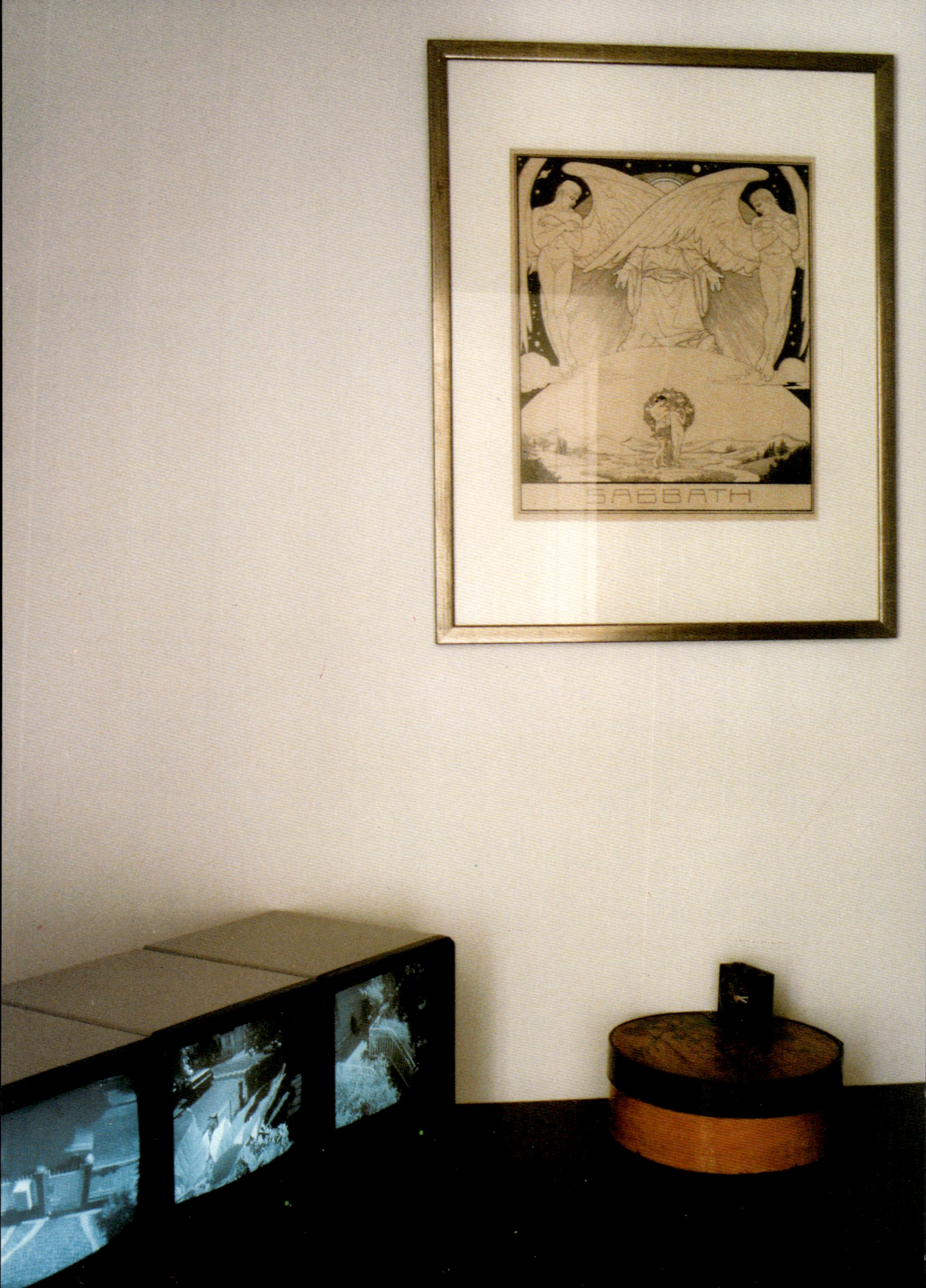
SABBATH

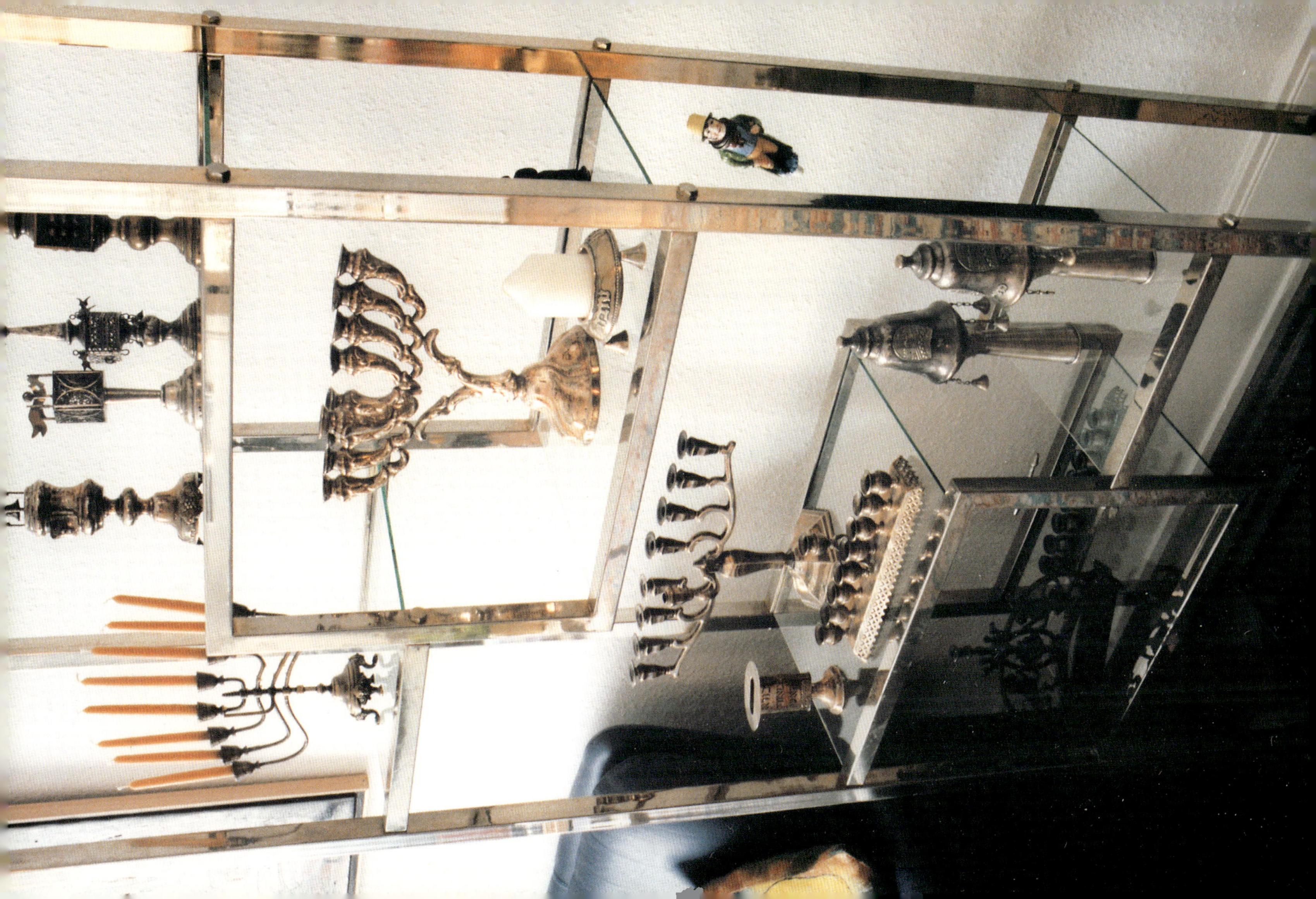

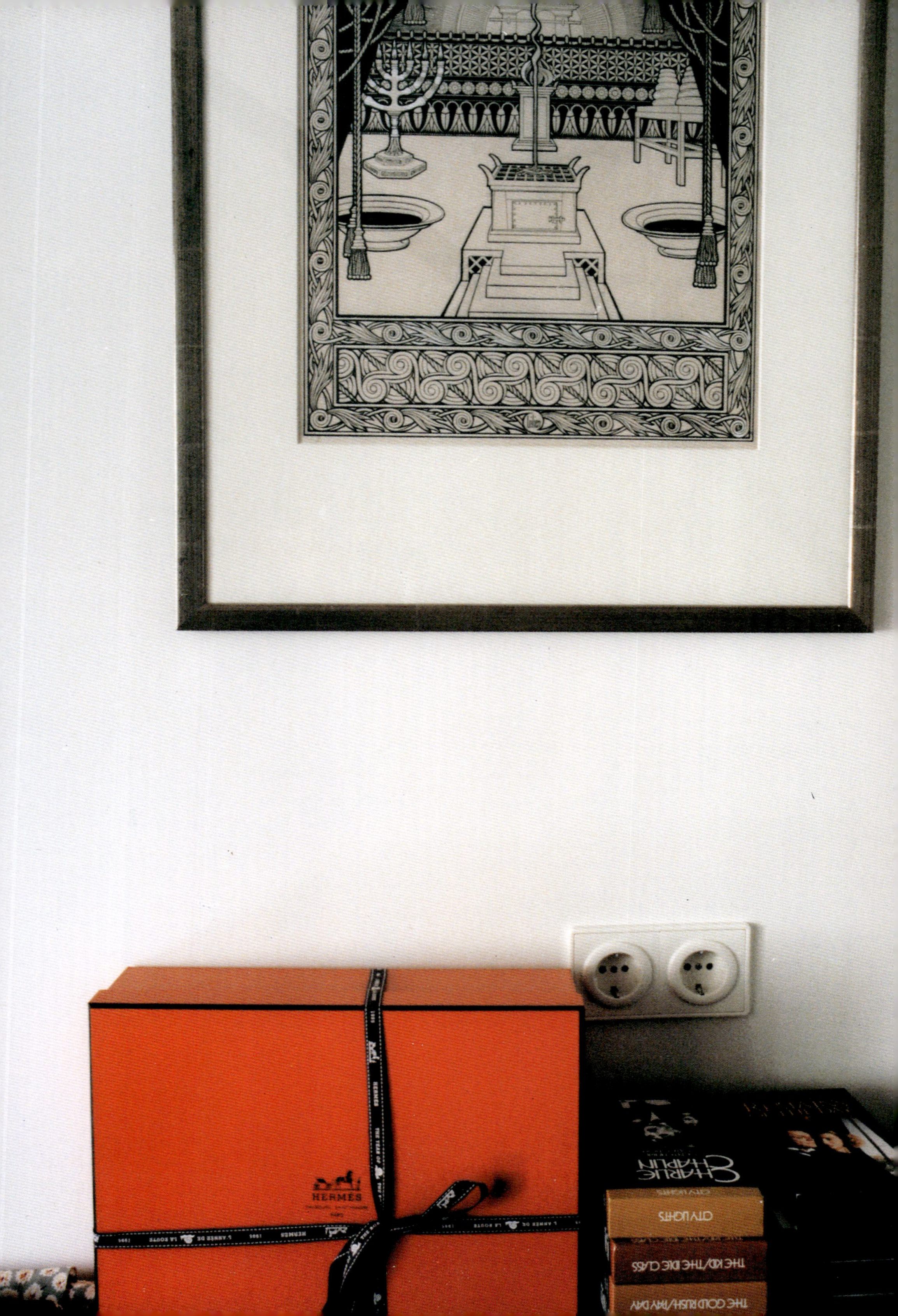

HERMES
PARIS
L'ANNÉE DE LA ROUTE
CHARLIE CHAPLIN
CITY LIGHTS
THE KID/THE IDLE CLASS
THE GOLD RUSH/PAY DAY

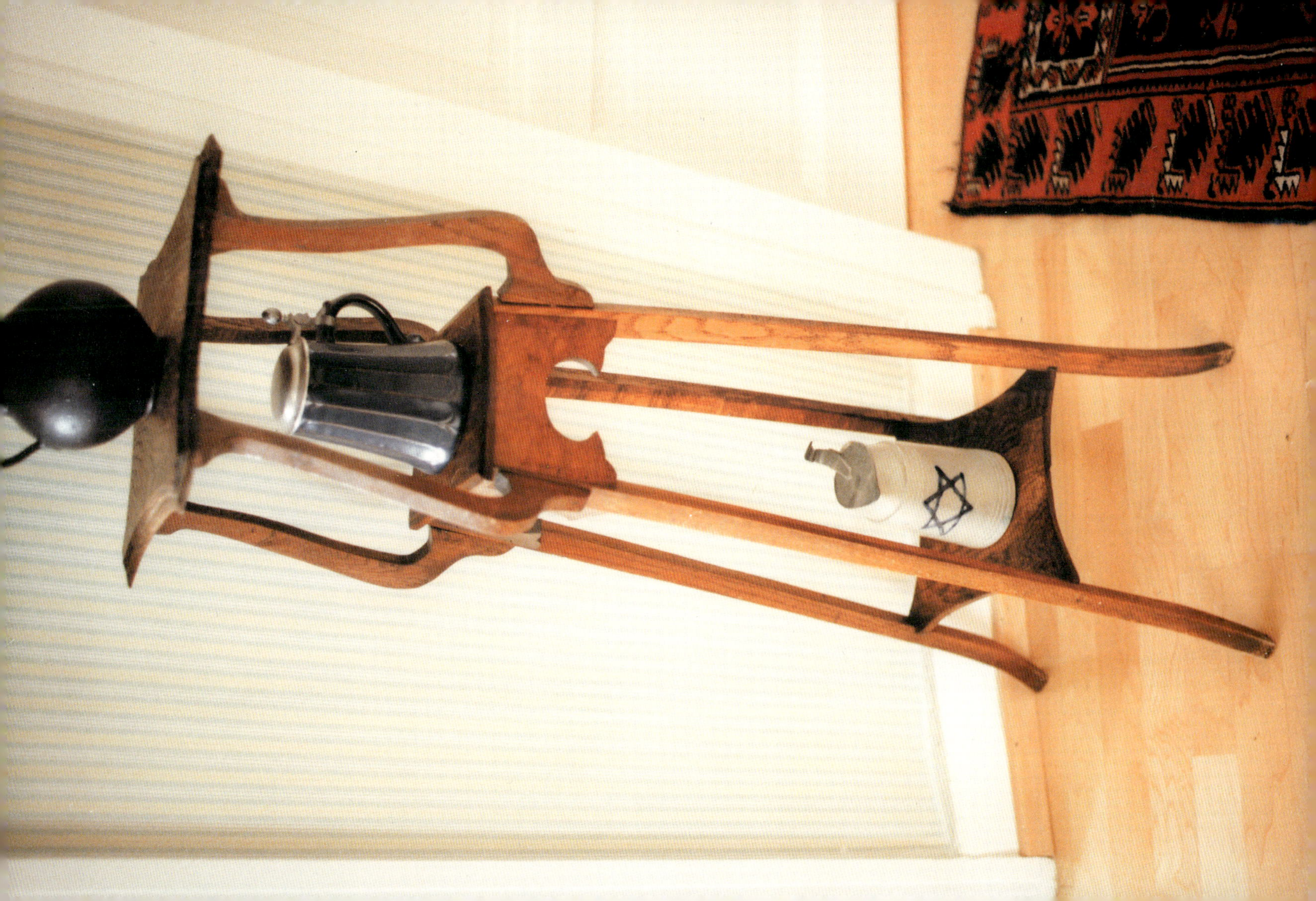

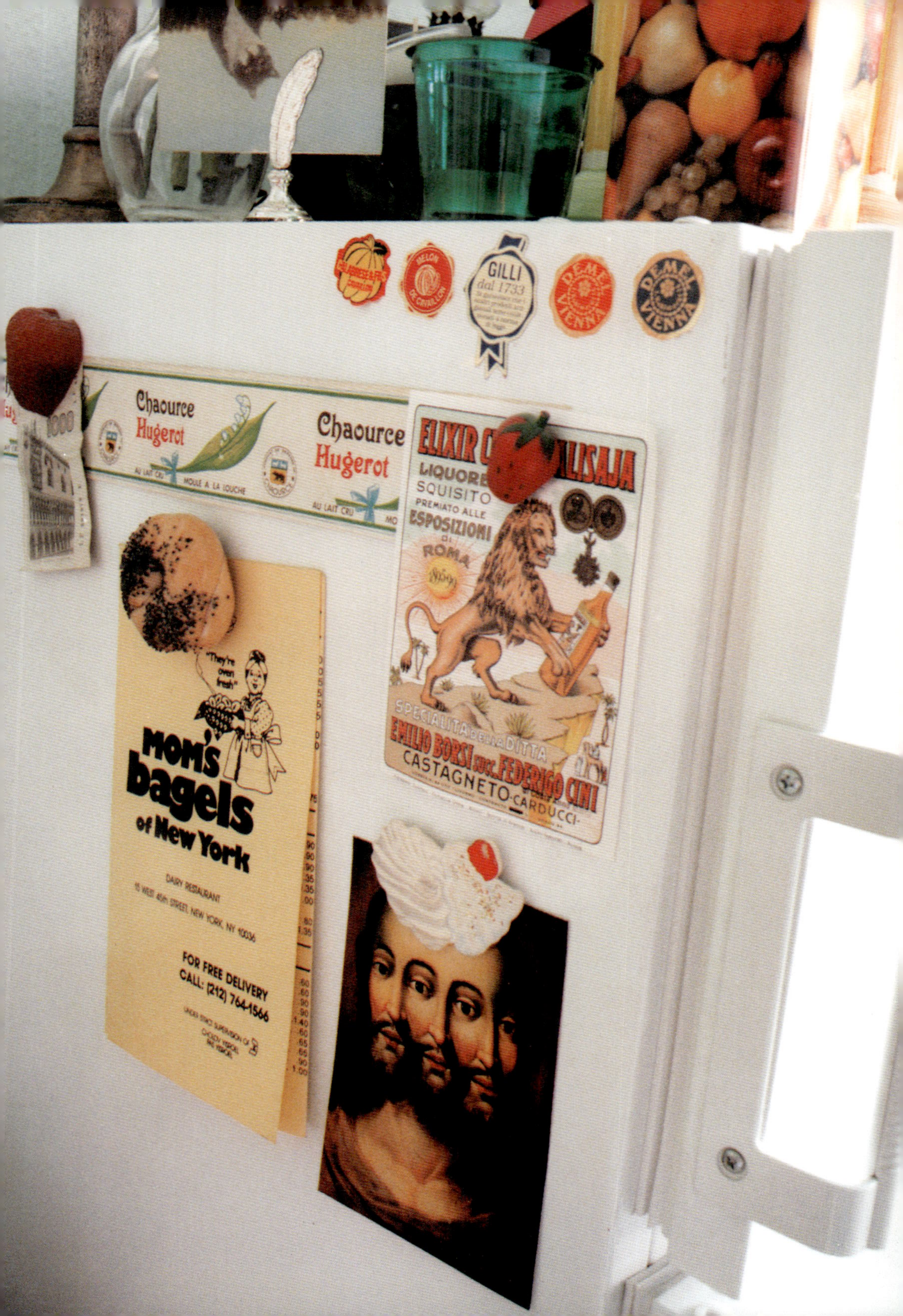
DEMEL VIENNA
DEMEL VIENNA
GILLI dal 1733
MELON DE CHARLEON
Chaource Hugerot
AU LAIT CRU
MOULE A LA LOUCHE
Chaource Hugerot
AU LAIT CRU
ELIXIR C... ALISAJA
LIQUORE SQUISITO
PREMIATO ALLE
ESPOSIZIONI
di ROMA
SPECIALITA DELLA DITTA
EMILIO BORSI succ. FEDERIGO CINI
CASTAGNETO-CARDUCCI
They're oven fresh!
mom's bagels
of New York
DAIRY RESTAURANT
15 WEST 45th STREET, NEW YORK, NY 10036
FOR FREE DELIVERY
CALL: (212) 764-1566

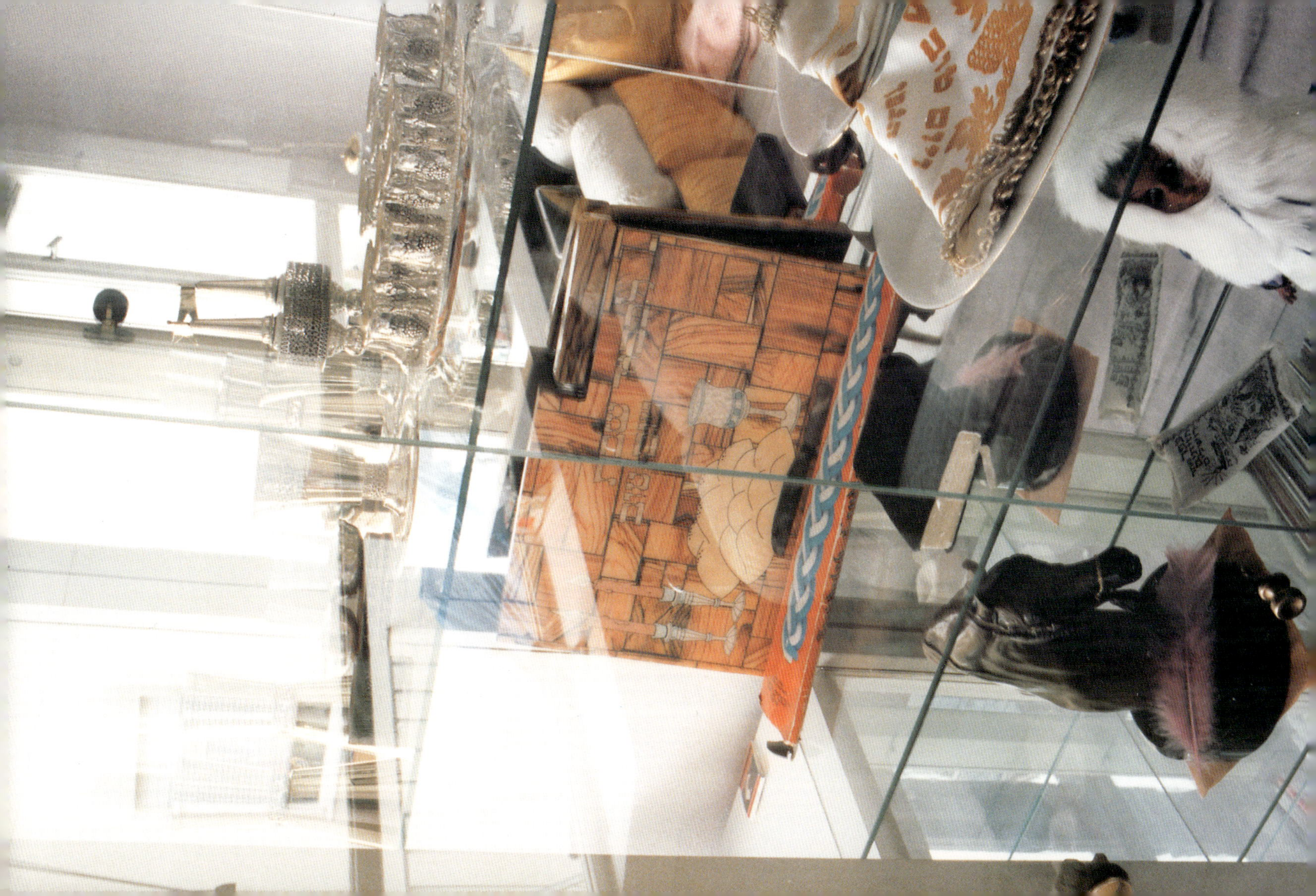

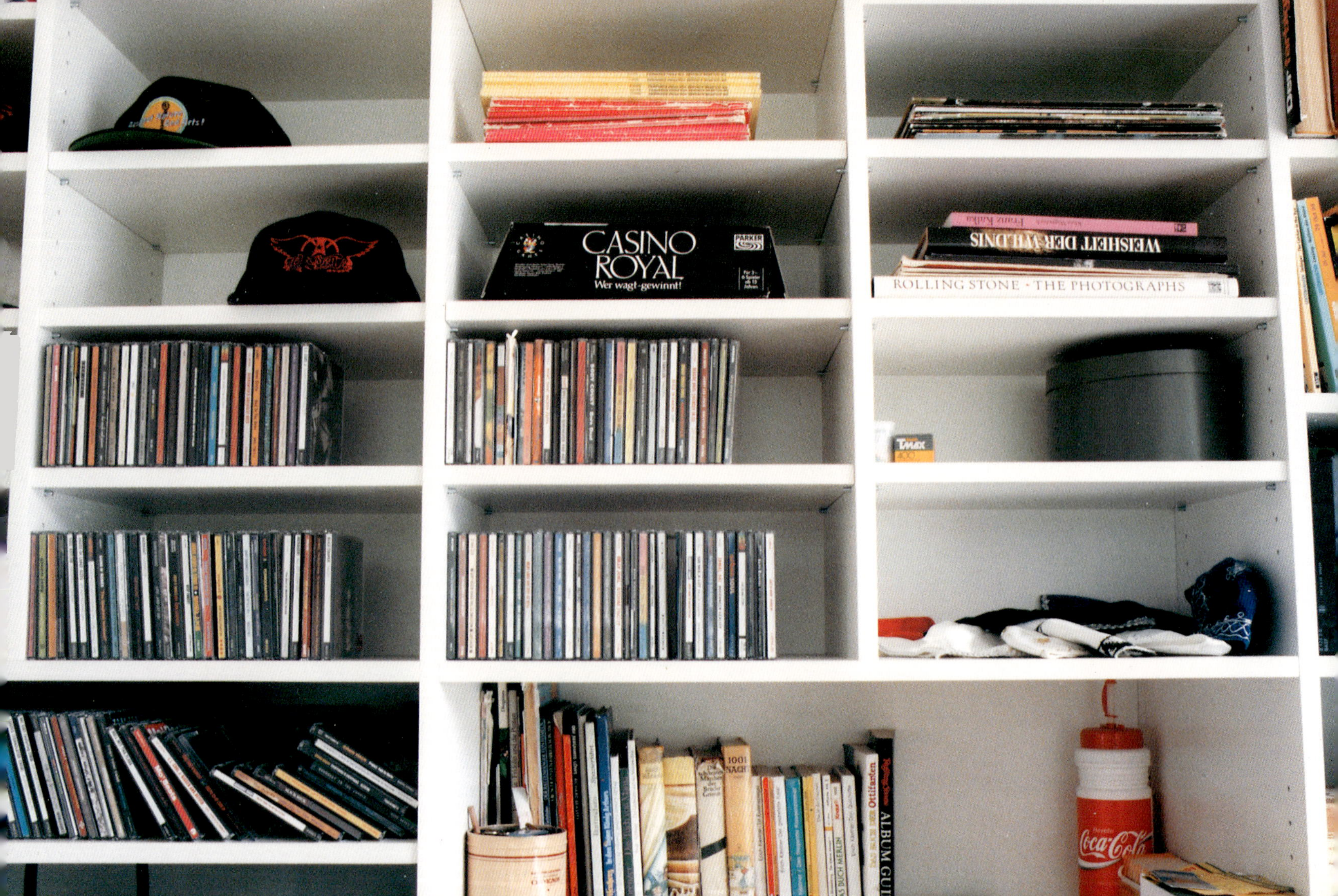
CASINO ROYAL
Wer wagt-gewinnt!
PARKER
WEISHEIT DER WILDNIS
ROLLING STONE · THE PHOTOGRAPHS
1001 NACHT
DAS BUCH MERLIN
ALBUM GUIDE
Coca-Cola

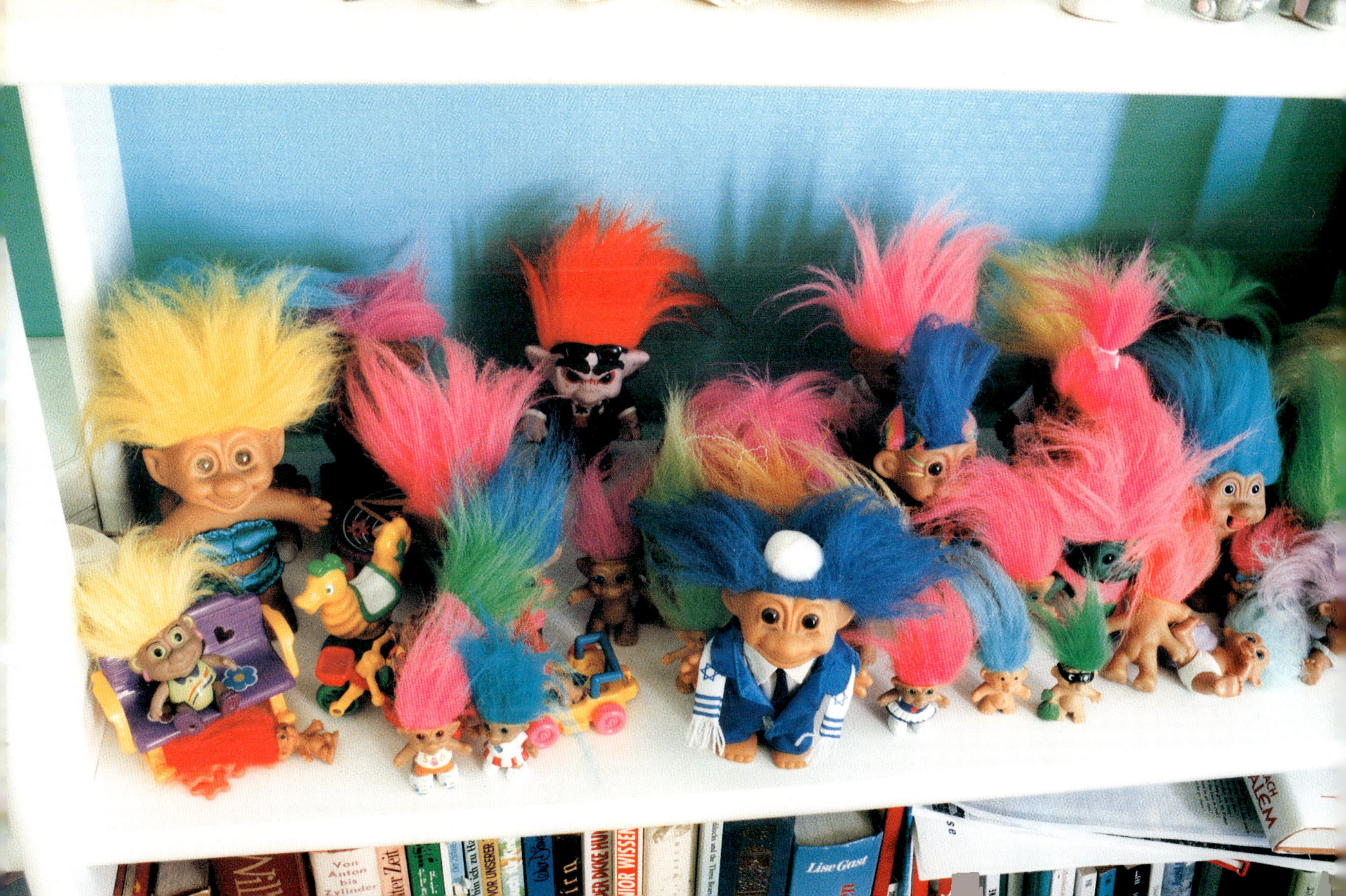

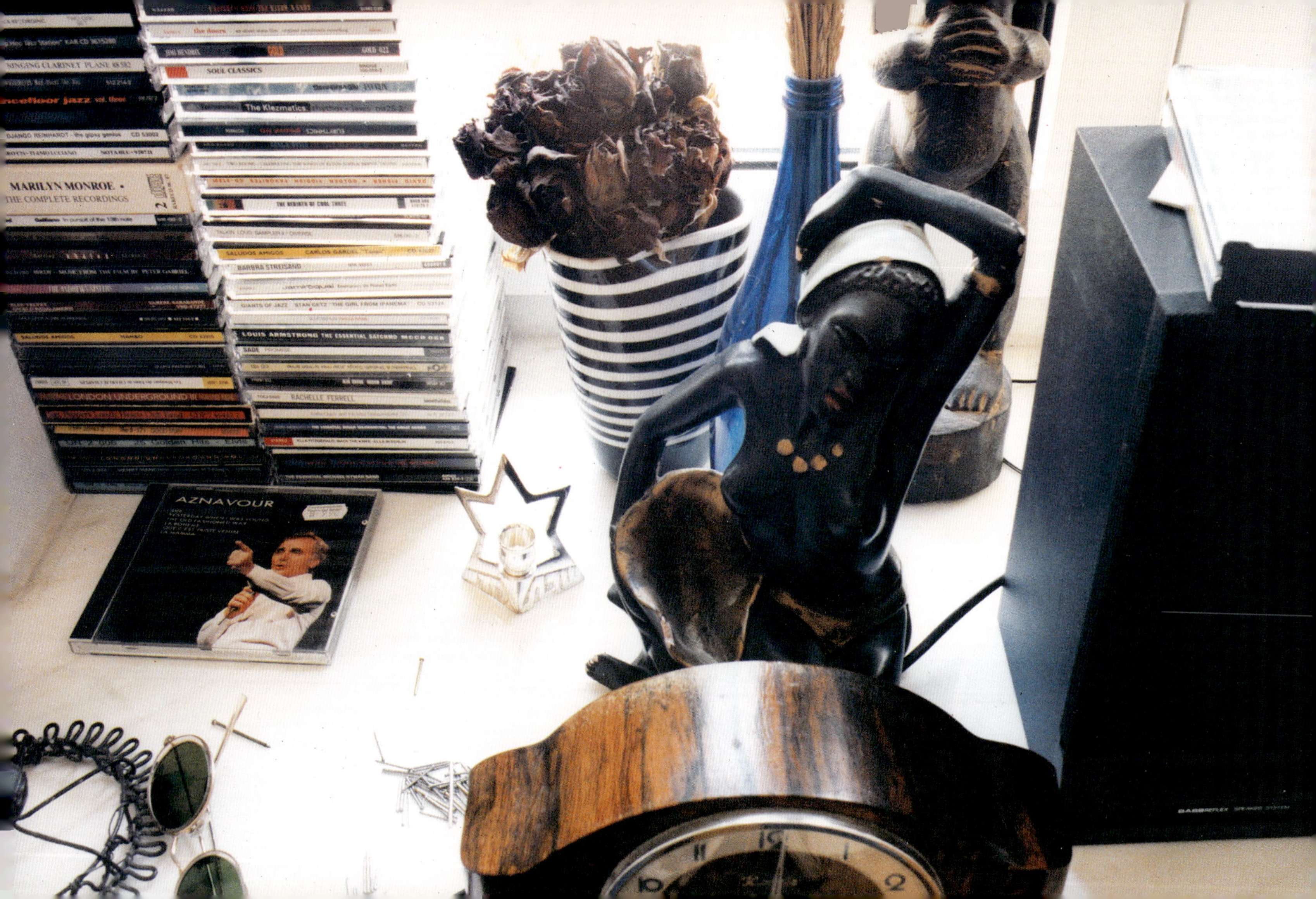

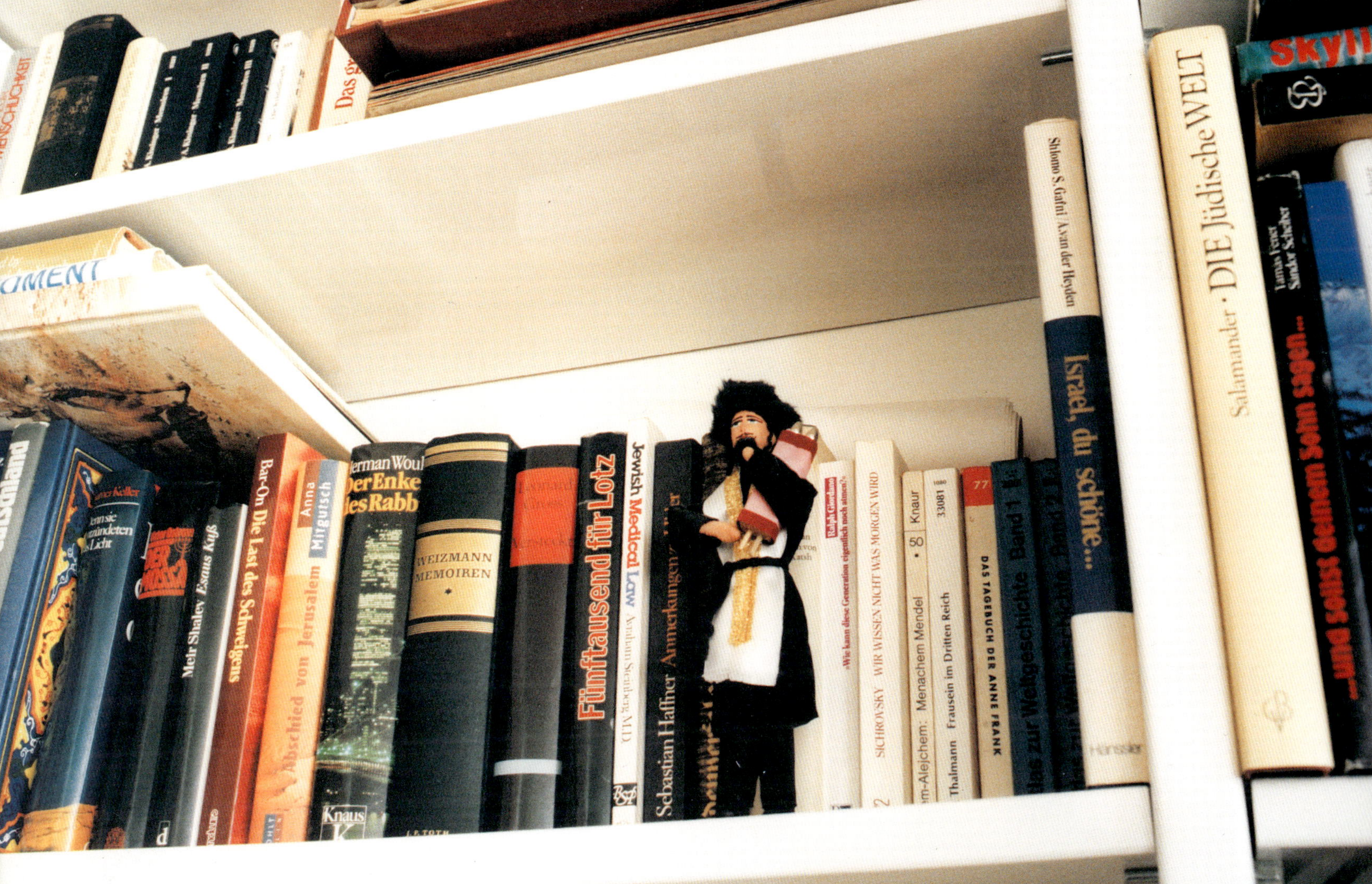
MENSCHGESCHICHTE
Das g...
Skyli...
DIE Jüdische WELT
Shlomo S. Gafni / A.van der Heyden
Israel, du schöne...
Salamander · DIE Jüdische WELT
Tamas Feiner Sandor Scheiber
...und sollst deinem Sohn sagen...
MOMENT
...eutschland
Wenn sie zündeten Licht
Meir Shalev Esaus Kuß
Bar-On Die Last des Schweigens
Anna Mitgutsch
Herman Wouk Der Enkel des Rabbi
WEIZMANN MEMOIREN
Abschied von Jerusalem
Fünftausend für Lotz
Jewish Medical Law Abraham Steinberg, M.D.
Sebastian Haffner Anmerkungen zu Hitler
Wie kann diese Generation eigentlich noch atmen?
Ralph Giordano
SICHROVSKY WIR WISSEN NICHT WAS MORGEN WIRD
...em-Alejchem: Menachem Mendel
Knaur 33081
50
Thalmann Frausein im Dritten Reich
DAS TAGEBUCH DER ANNE FRANK
Das zur Weltgeschichte Band 1
Hänssler
Knaus
J.P. TOTH

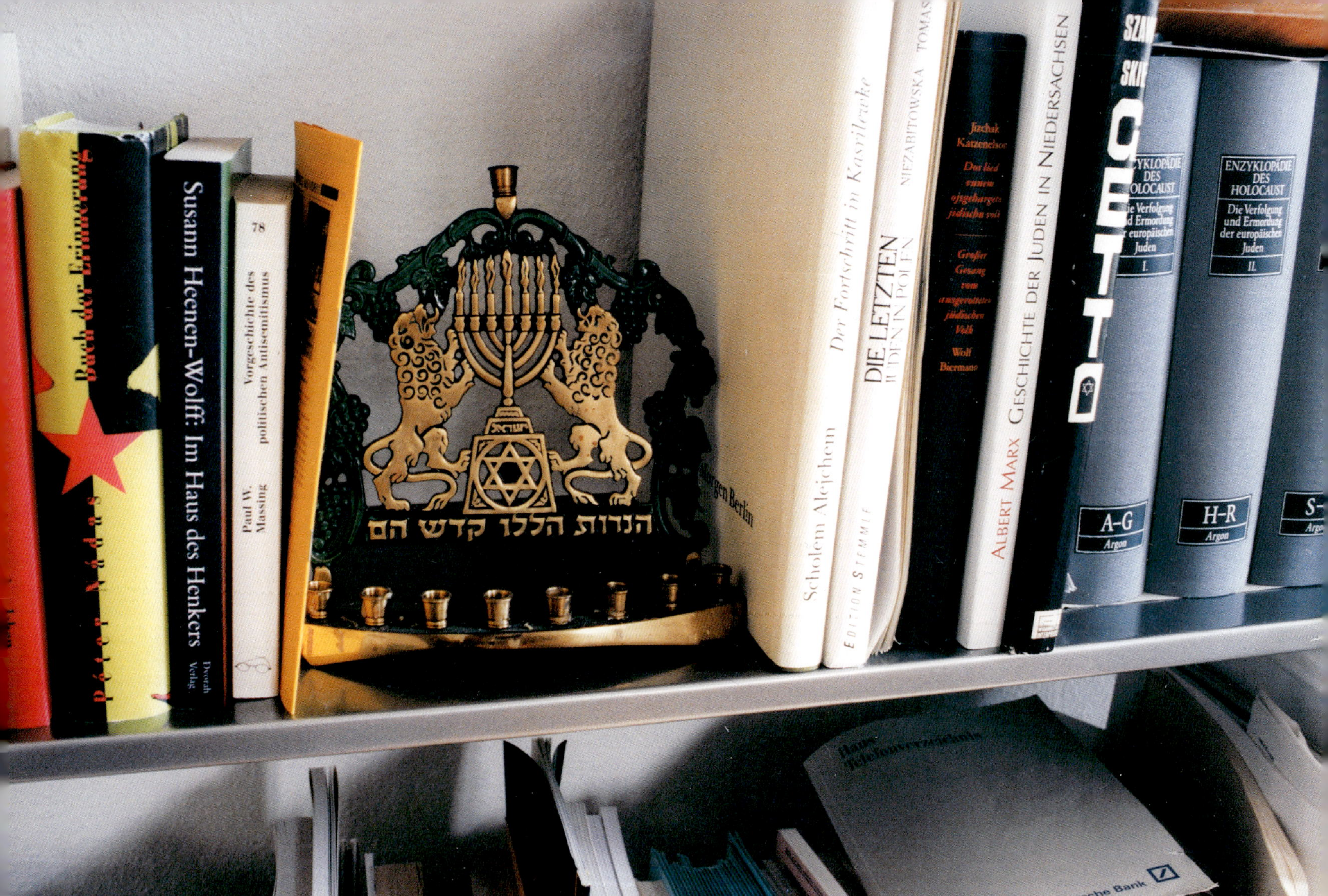

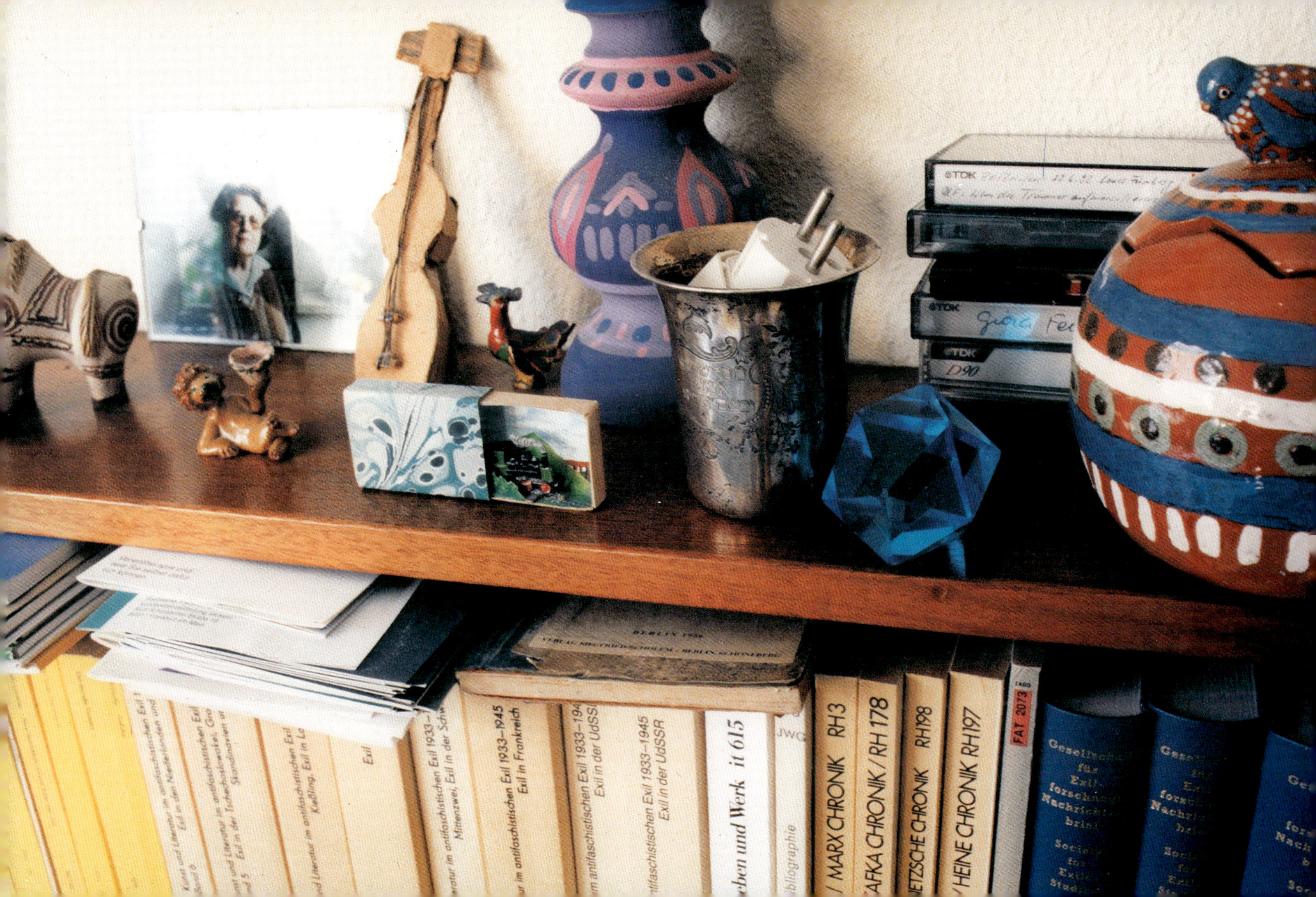
TDK D90
TDK
BERLIN 1936
VERLAG SIEGFRIED SCHOLEM · BERLIN-SCHÖNEBERG
Kunst und Literatur im antifaschistischen Exil
Exil in den Niederlanden und
Band 6
Kunst und Literatur im antifaschistischen Exil 1933–1945
Exil in der Tschechoslowakei, Großbritannien
Band 5 Exil in der Schweiz
Kießling, Exil in London
Literatur im antifaschistischen Exil
Mittenzwei, Exil in der Schweiz
Kunst und Literatur im antifaschistischen Exil 1933–1945
Exil in Frankreich
Kunst und Literatur im antifaschistischen Exil 1933–1945
Exil in der UdSSR
Kunst und Literatur im antifaschistischen Exil 1933–1945
Exil in der UdSSR
Leben und Werk it 615
Bibliographie JWG
/ MARX CHRONIK RH 3
KAFKA CHRONIK / RH 178
NIETZSCHE CHRONIK RH198
/ HEINE CHRONIK RH197
FAT 2073
Gesellschaft für Exilforschung Nachrichtenbrief
Society for Exile Studies
Gesellschaft für Exilforschung Nachrichtenbrief

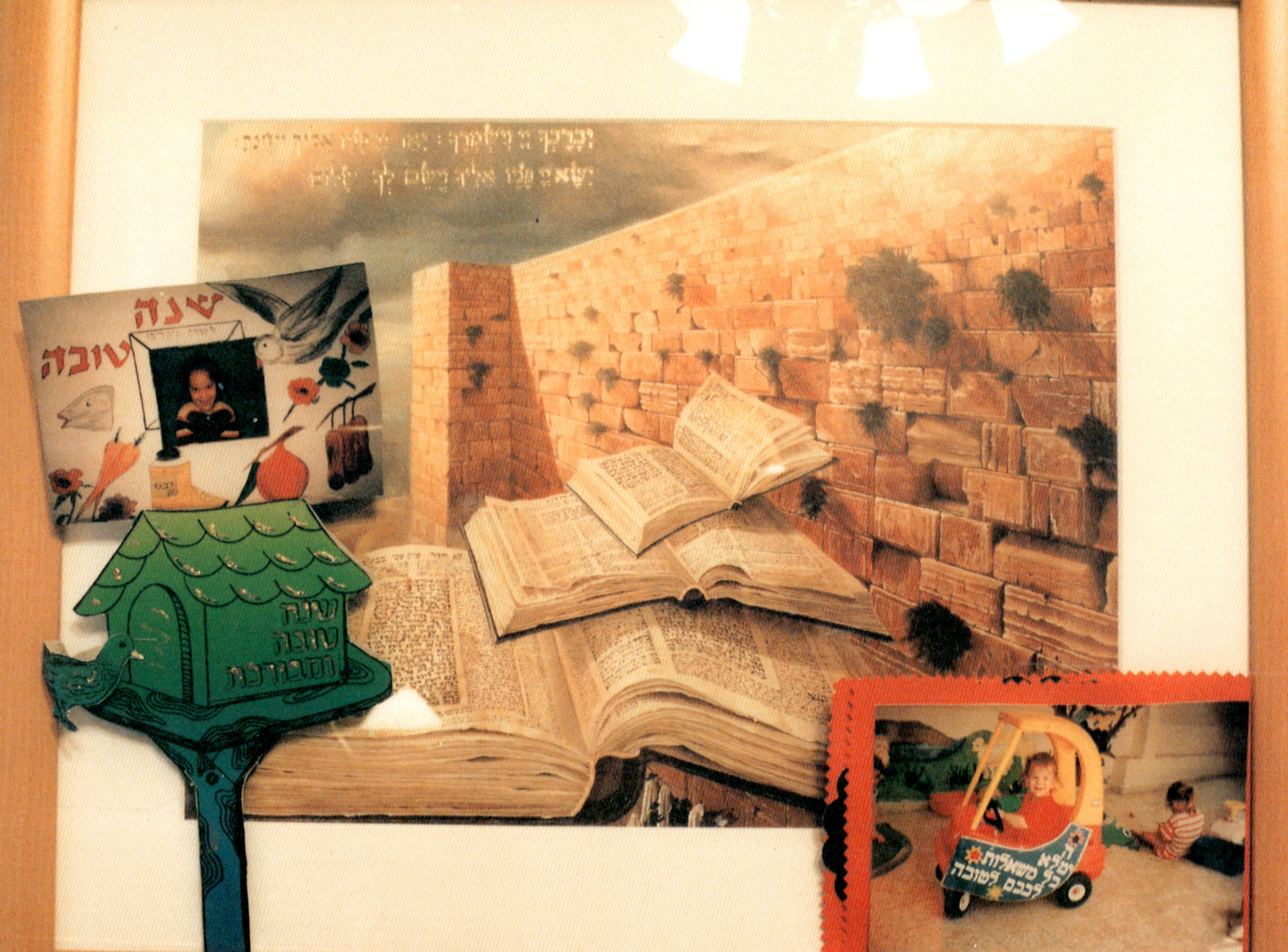

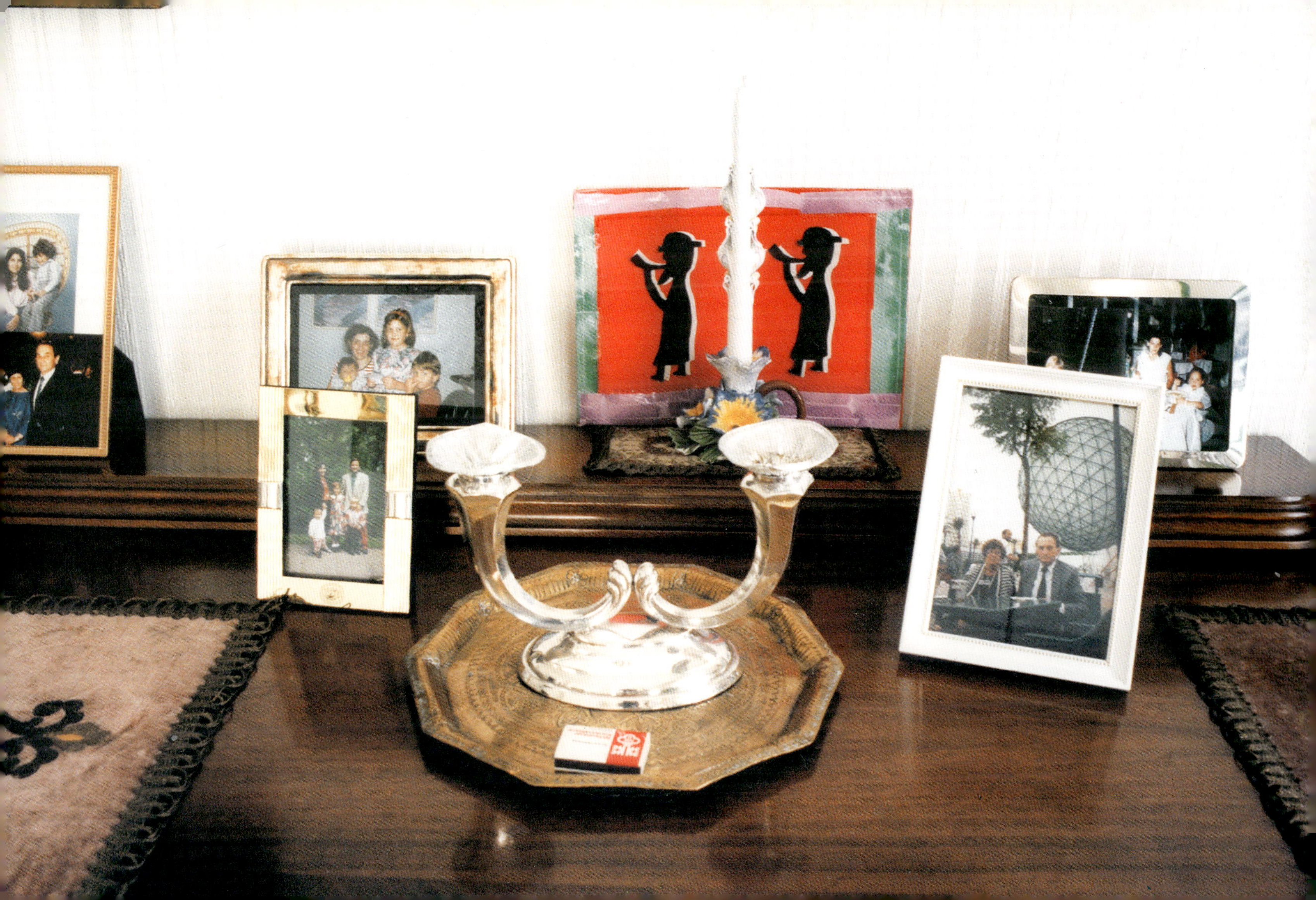

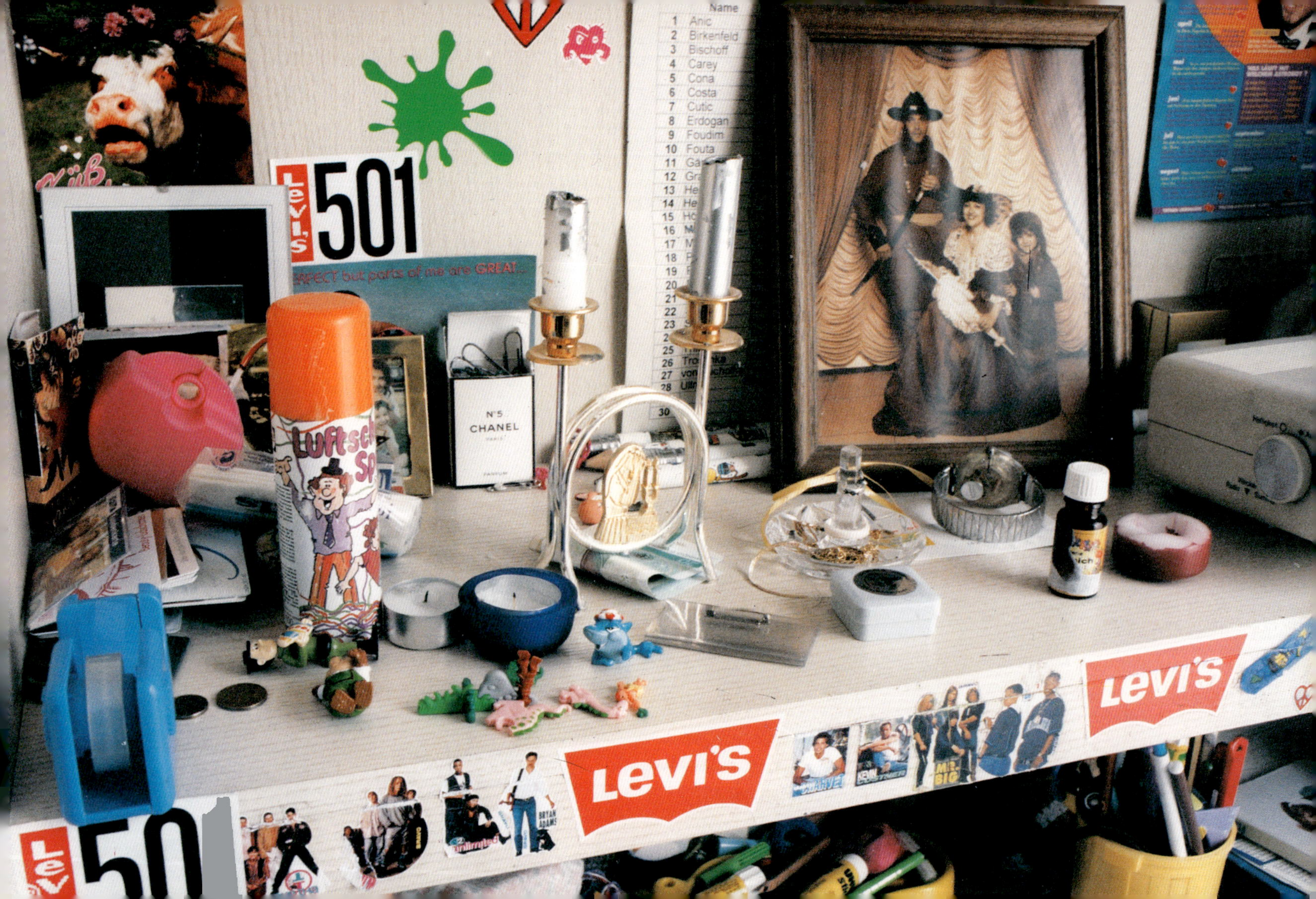
501
LEVI'S
...PECT but parts of me are GREAT...
N°5 CHANEL PARIS PARFUM
Luftschlangen SP
Name
1 Anic
2 Birkenfeld
3 Bischoff
4 Carey
5 Cona
6 Costa
7 Cutic
8 Erdogan
9 Foudim
10 Fouta
11 Ga
12 Gr
13 He
14 He
15 Ho
16 M
17 M
18 P
19 P
20
21
22
23
25
26 Tro ka
27 von ch
28 Ultr
30
Levi's
Levi's
MR. BIG
BRYAN ADAMS
unlimited

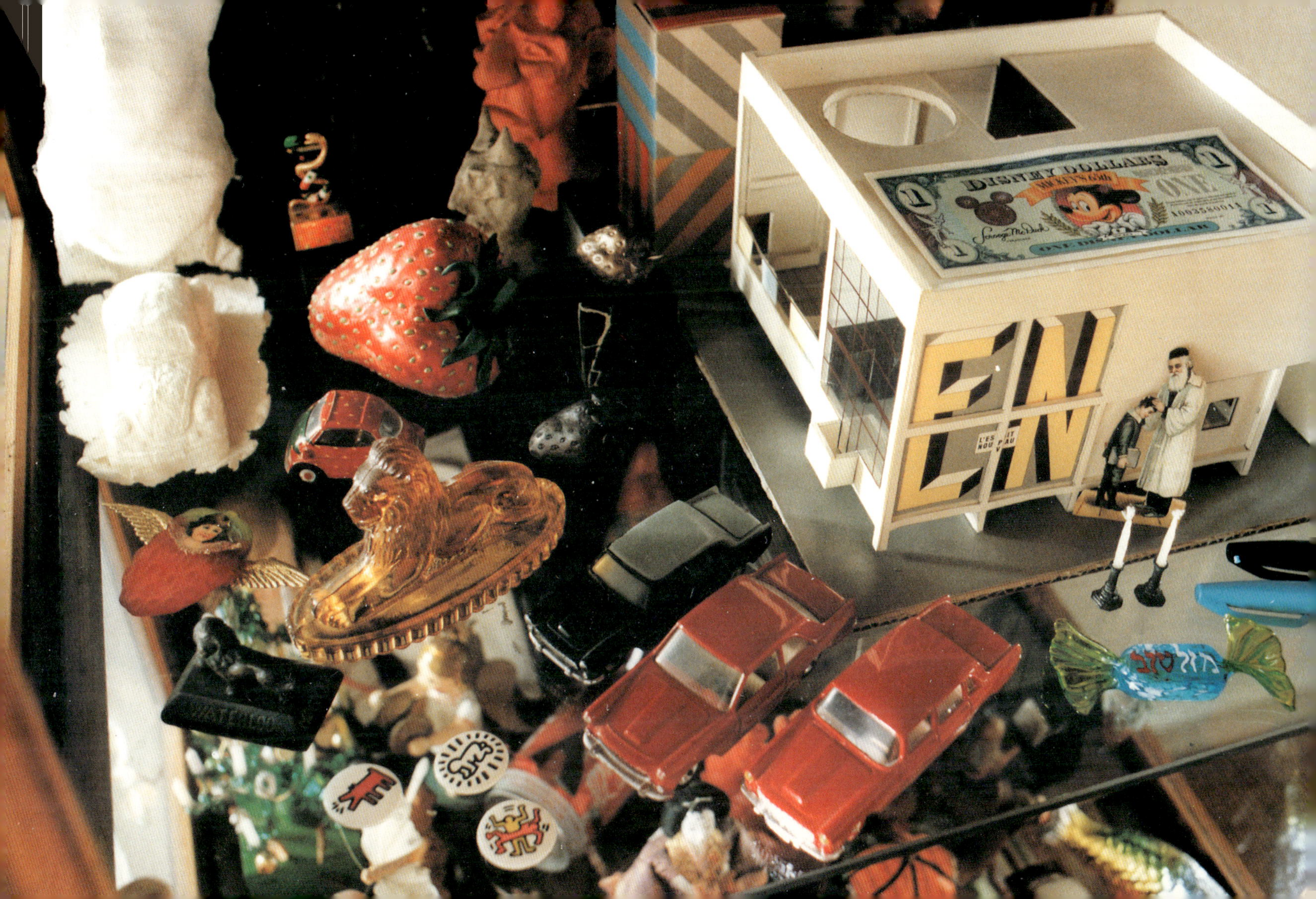

DISNEY DOLLARS
ONE
MICKEY'S GOLD
Scrooge McDuck
ONE DISNEY DOLLAR
EN
LN
L'ES AT
NOU P AU
WATERLOO

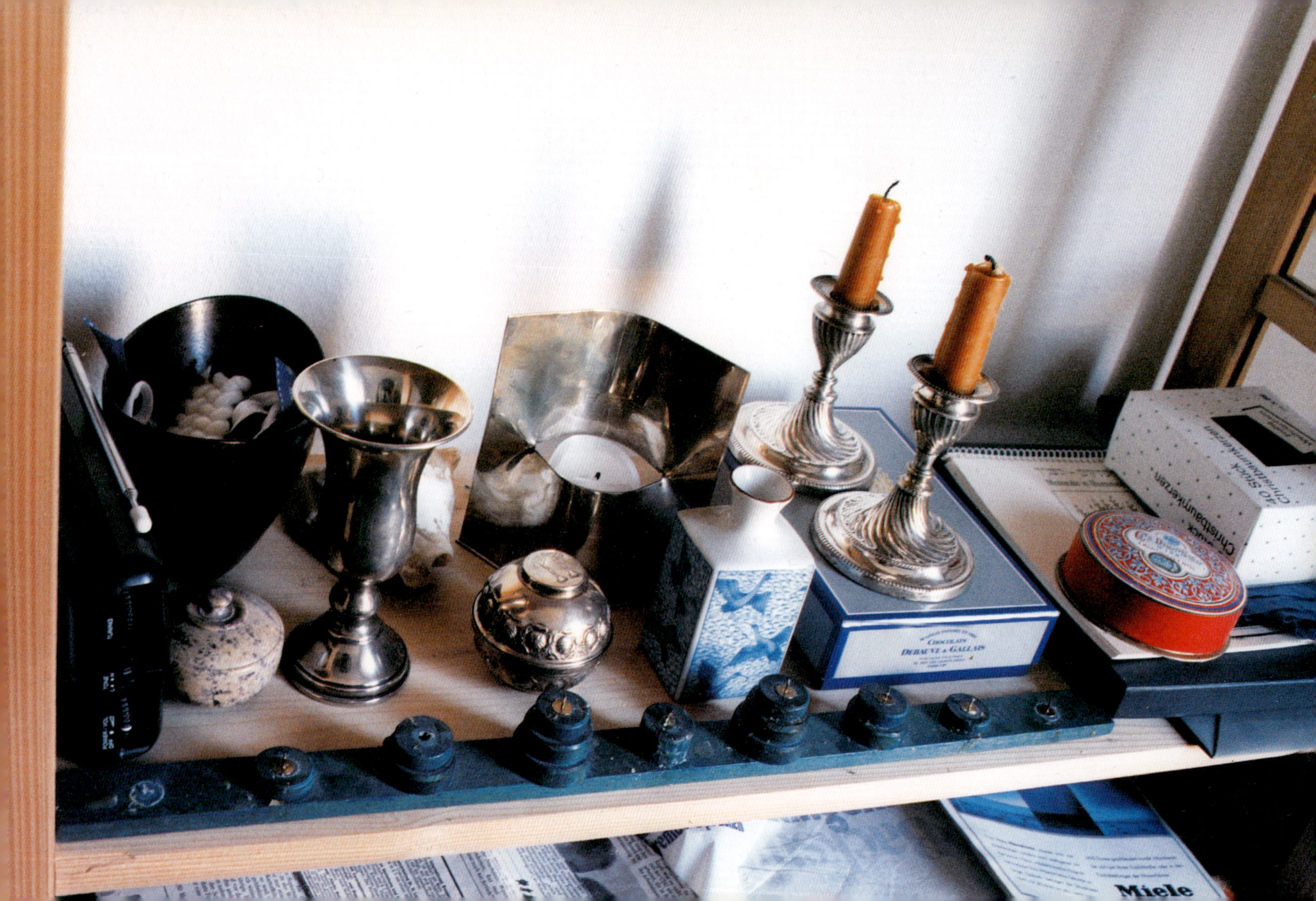
CHOCOLATS
DEBAUVE & GALLAIS
20 Stück
Christbaumkerzen
Miele

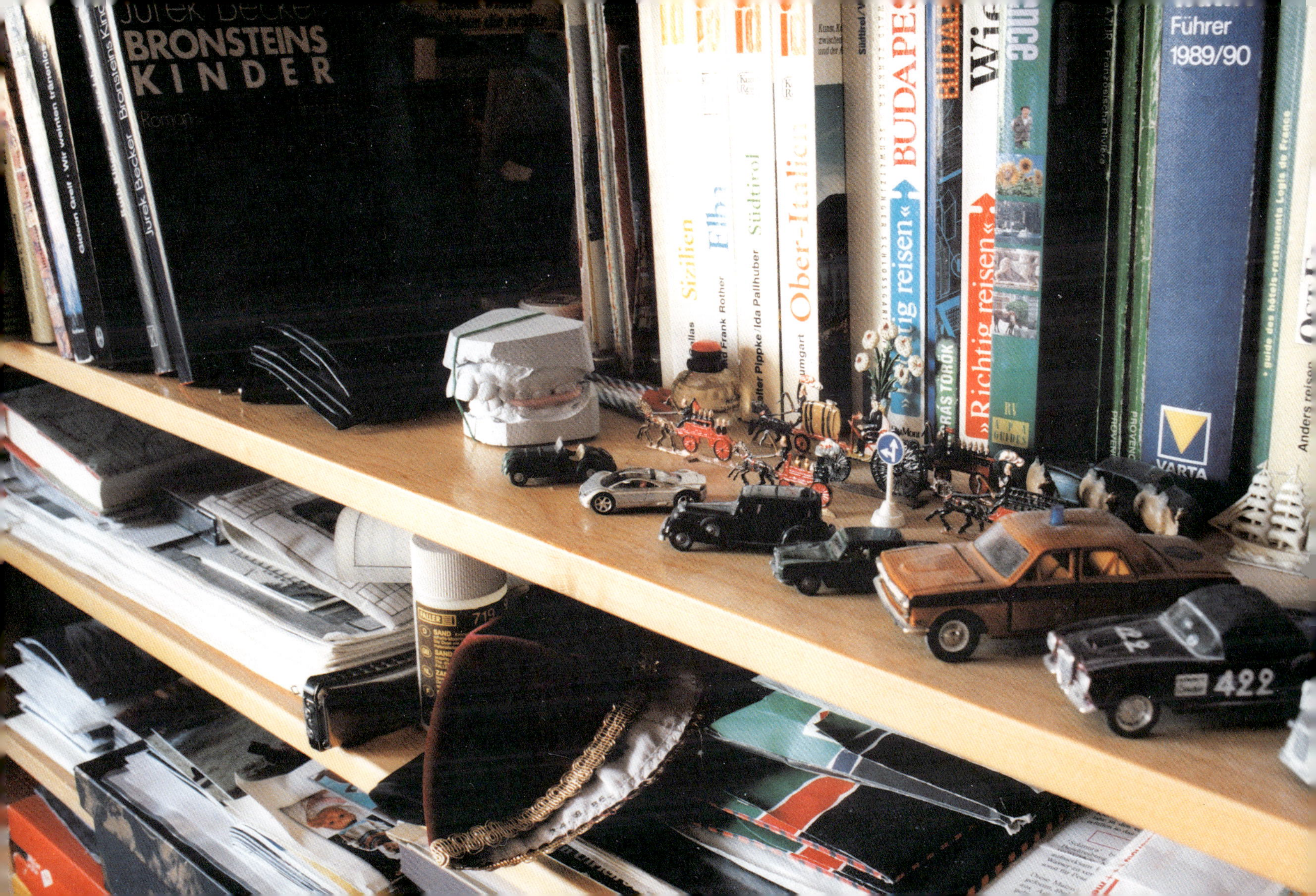

Jurek Becker
BRONSTEINS KINDER
Roman
Sizilien
Südtirol
Ober-Italien
BUDAPEST
richtig reisen
richtig reisen
Führer
1989/90
VARTA
FALLER

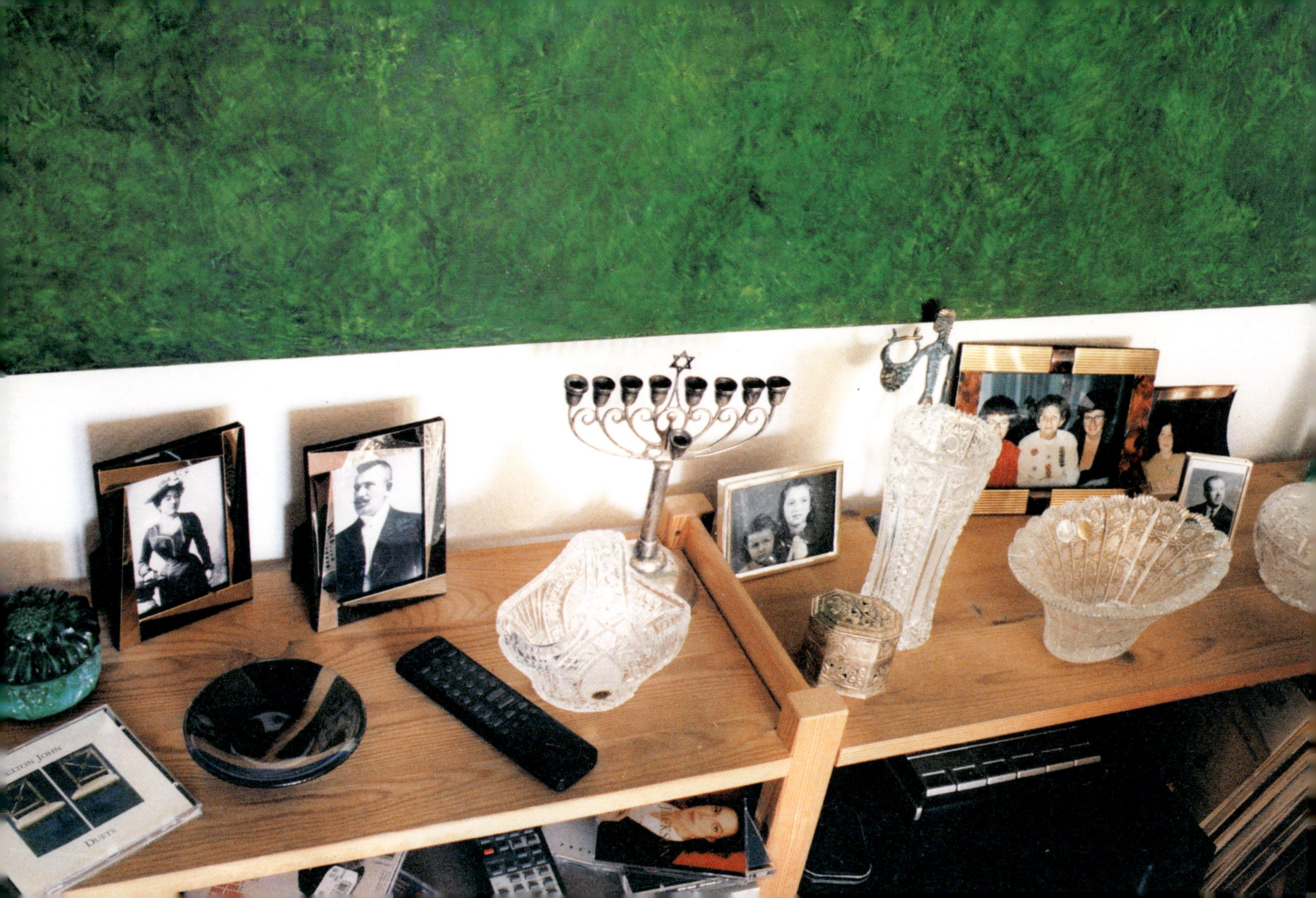

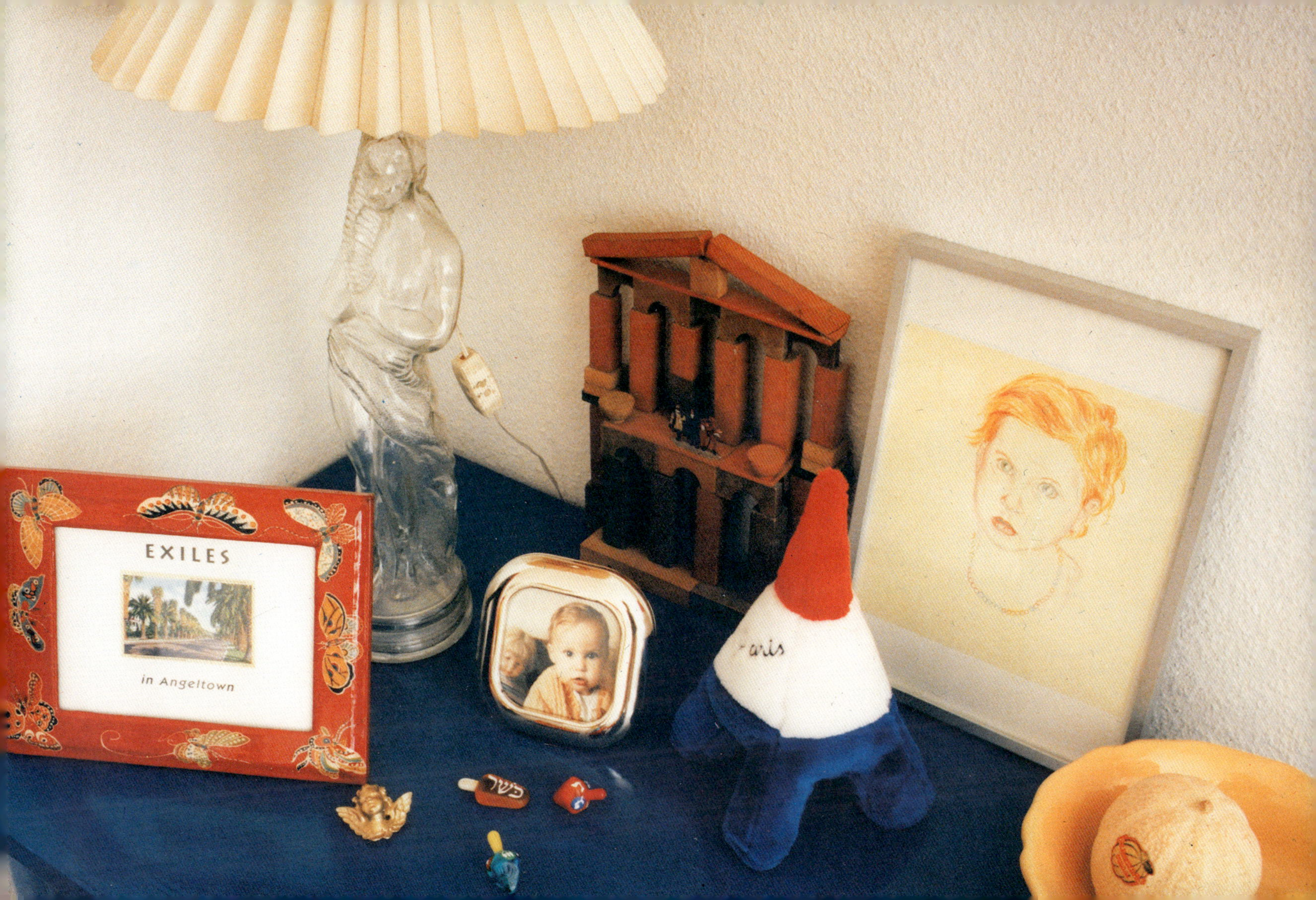

EXILES
in Angeltown
Paris

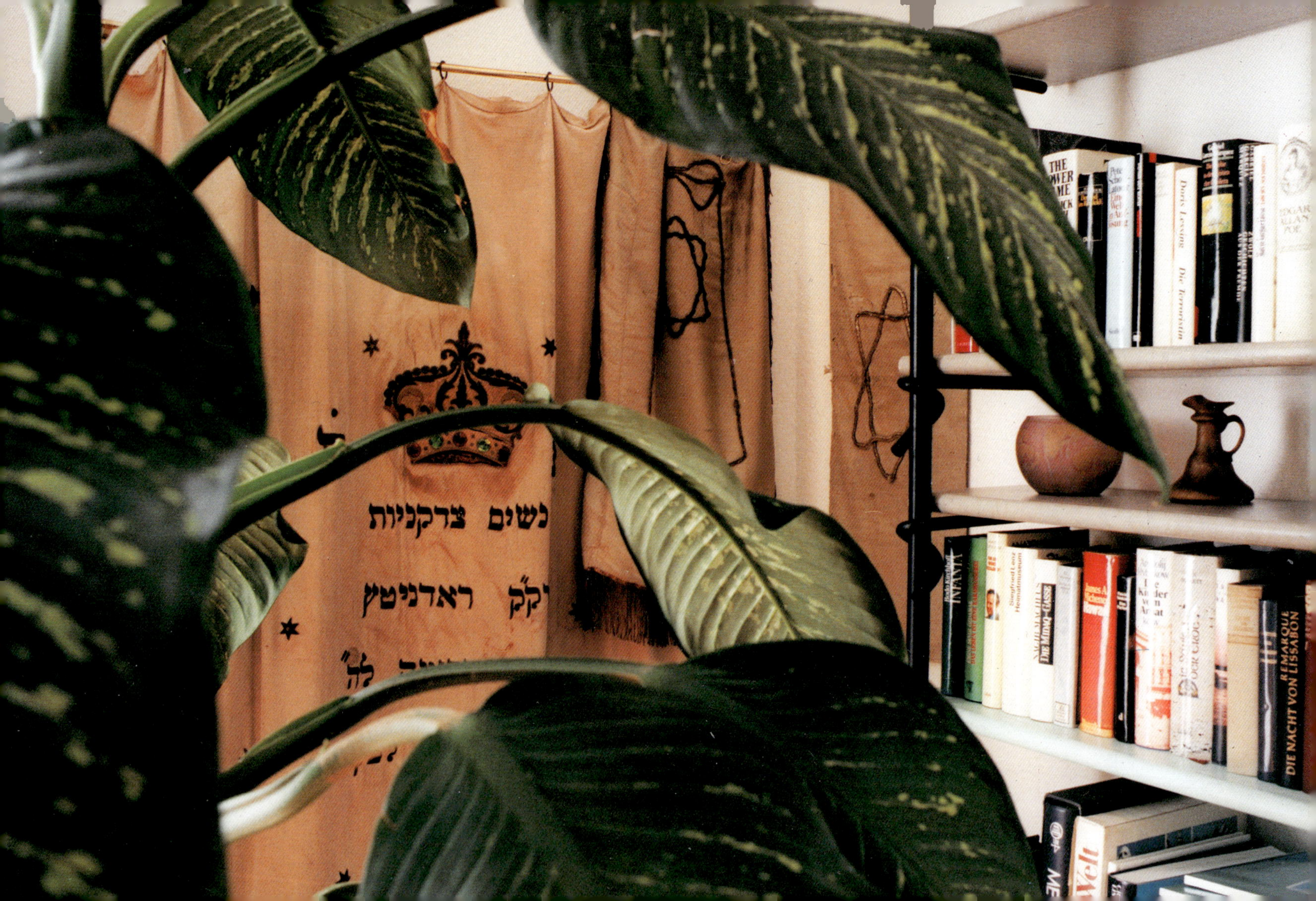

נשים ברכניות
יק"ק ראדניץ

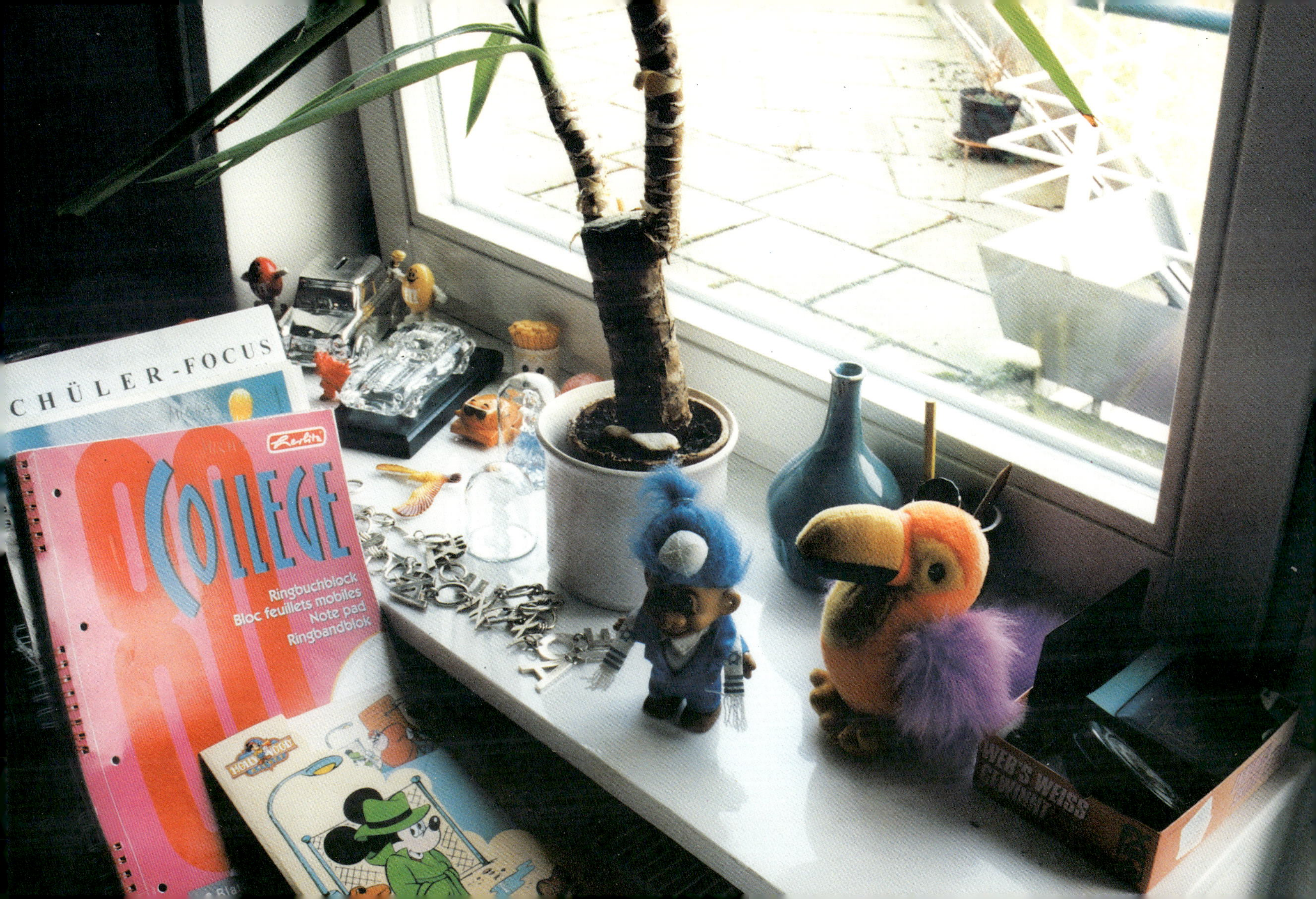
CHÜLER-FOCUS
Herlitz
COLLEGE
Ringbuchblock
Bloc feuillets mobiles
Note pad
Ringbandblok
HOLLYWOOD
WER'S WEISS

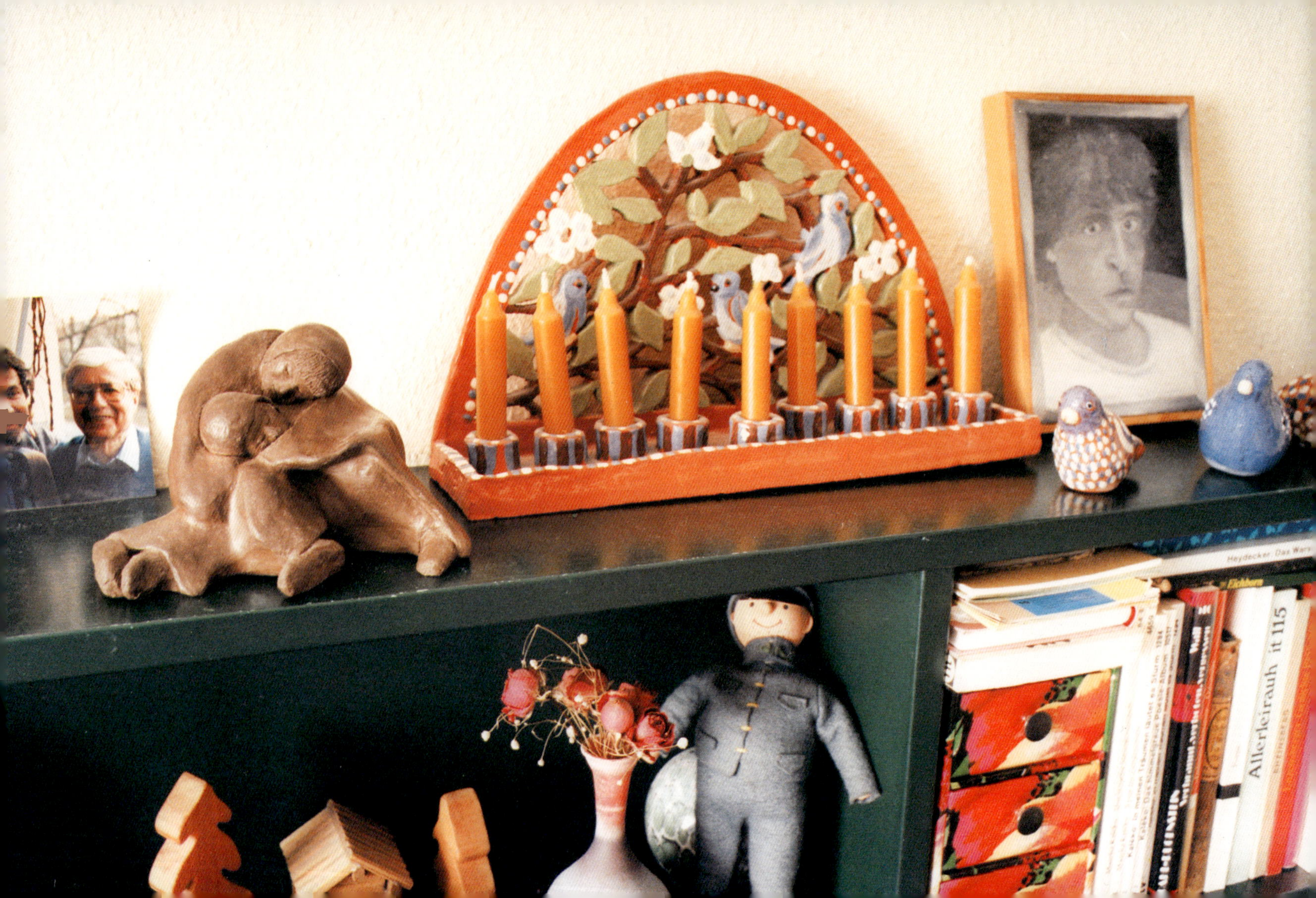

Heydecker: Das War...
Eichborn
Allerleirauh it 115

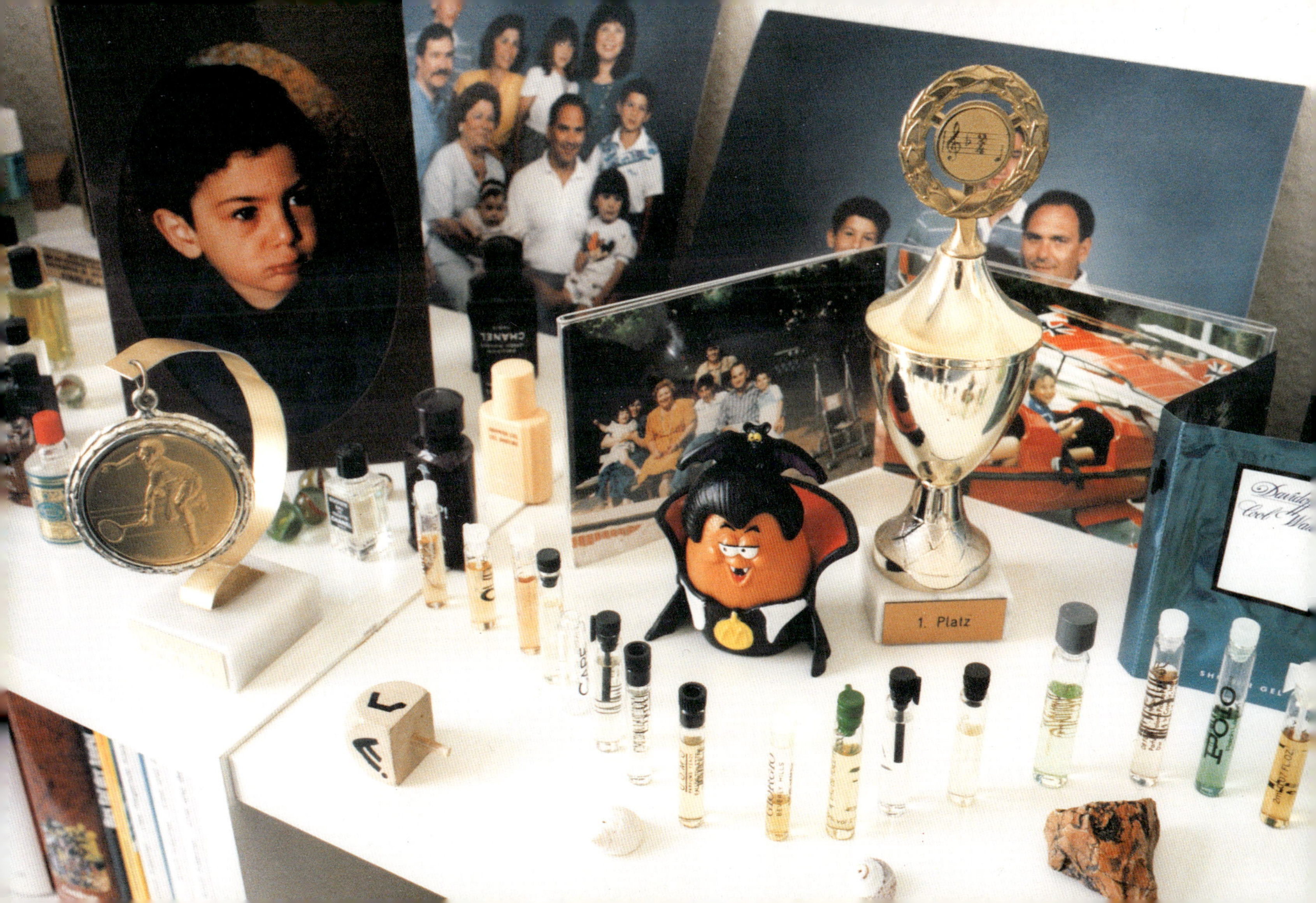

CHANEL
1. Platz
POLO
Davidoff
Cool Water
SHOWER GEL

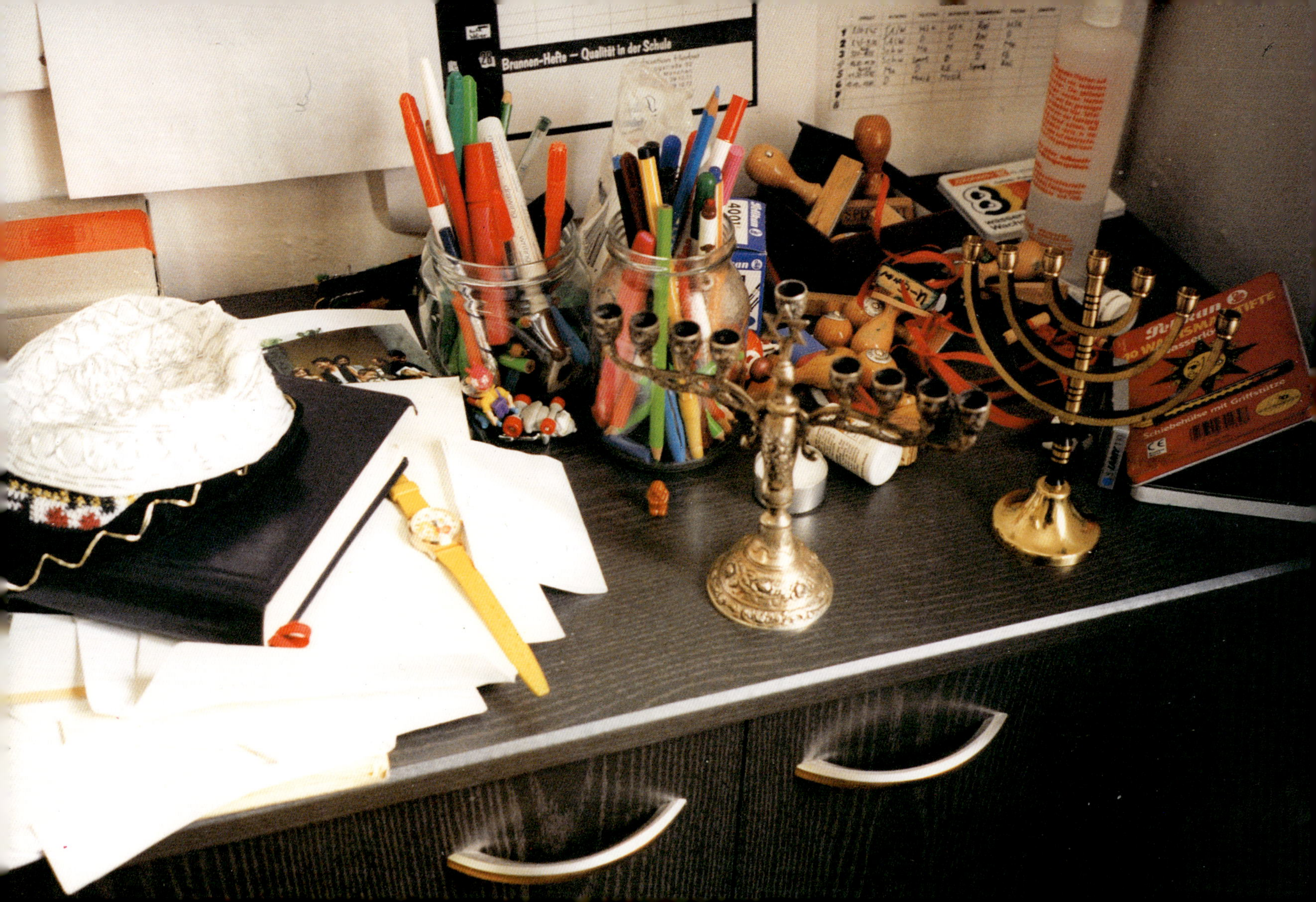

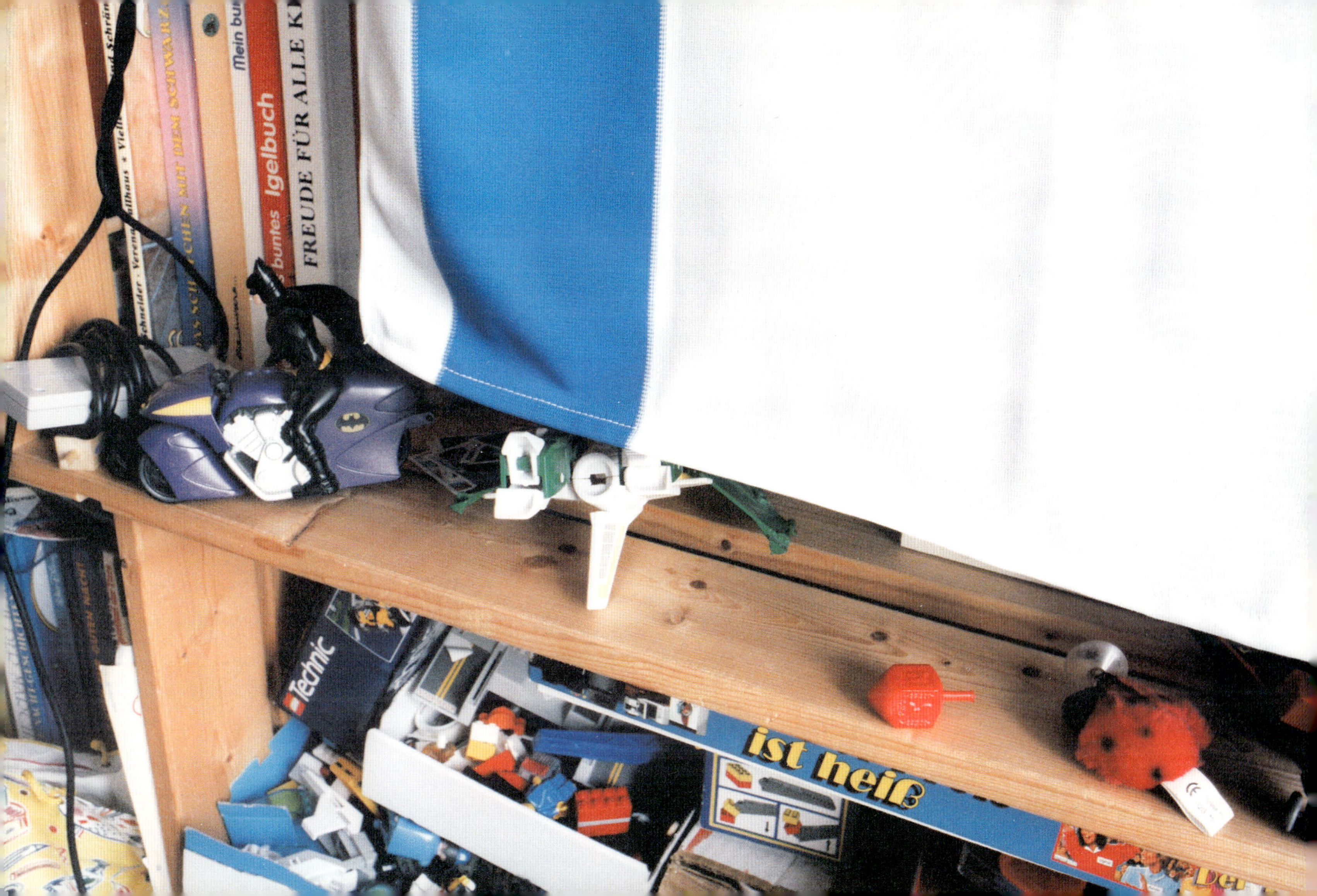

Mein buntes Igelbuch
FREUDE FÜR ALLE K
DAS SCHLÖSSCHEN MIT DEM SCHWARZ
Technic
ist heiß

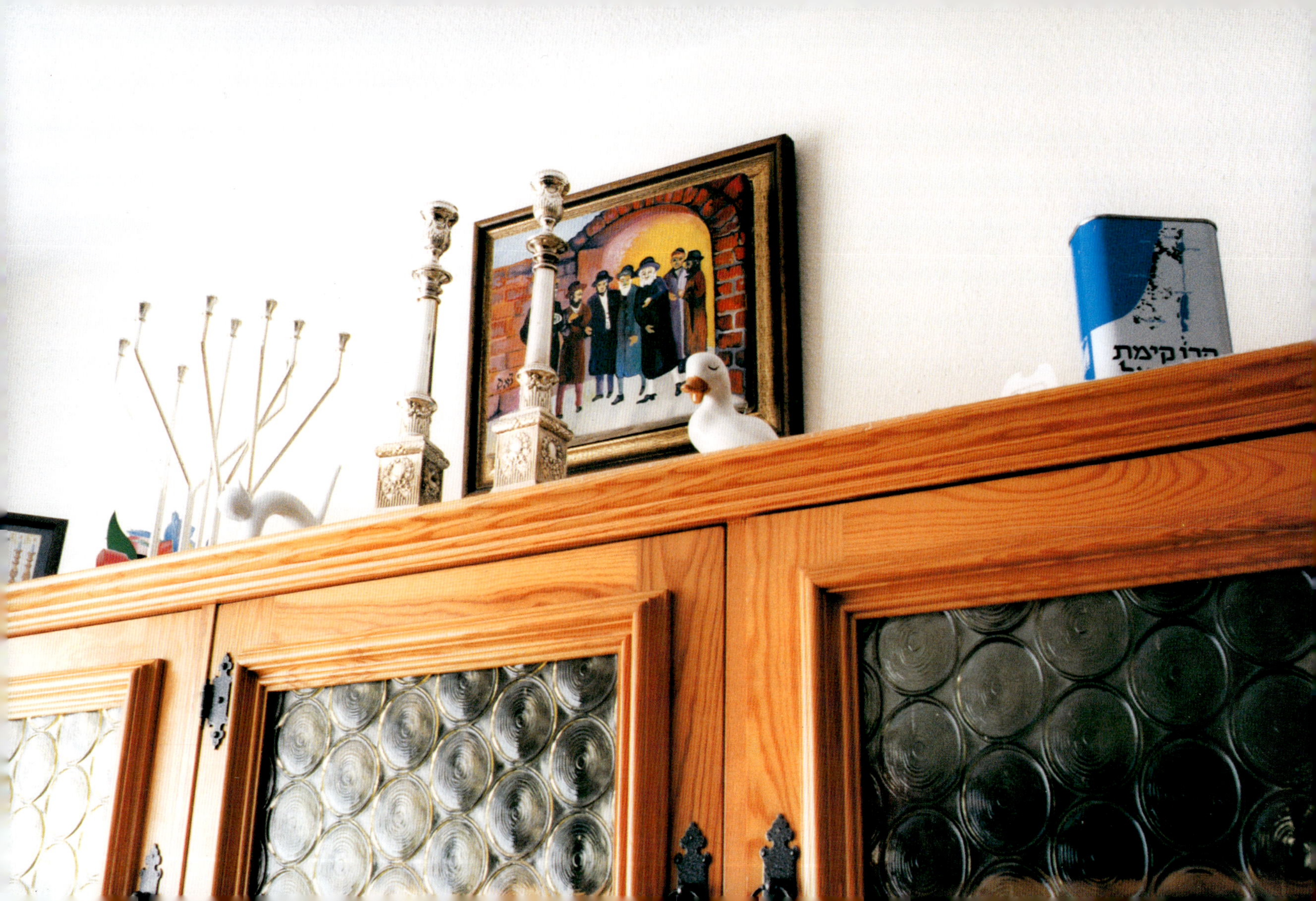
קימת
הרו

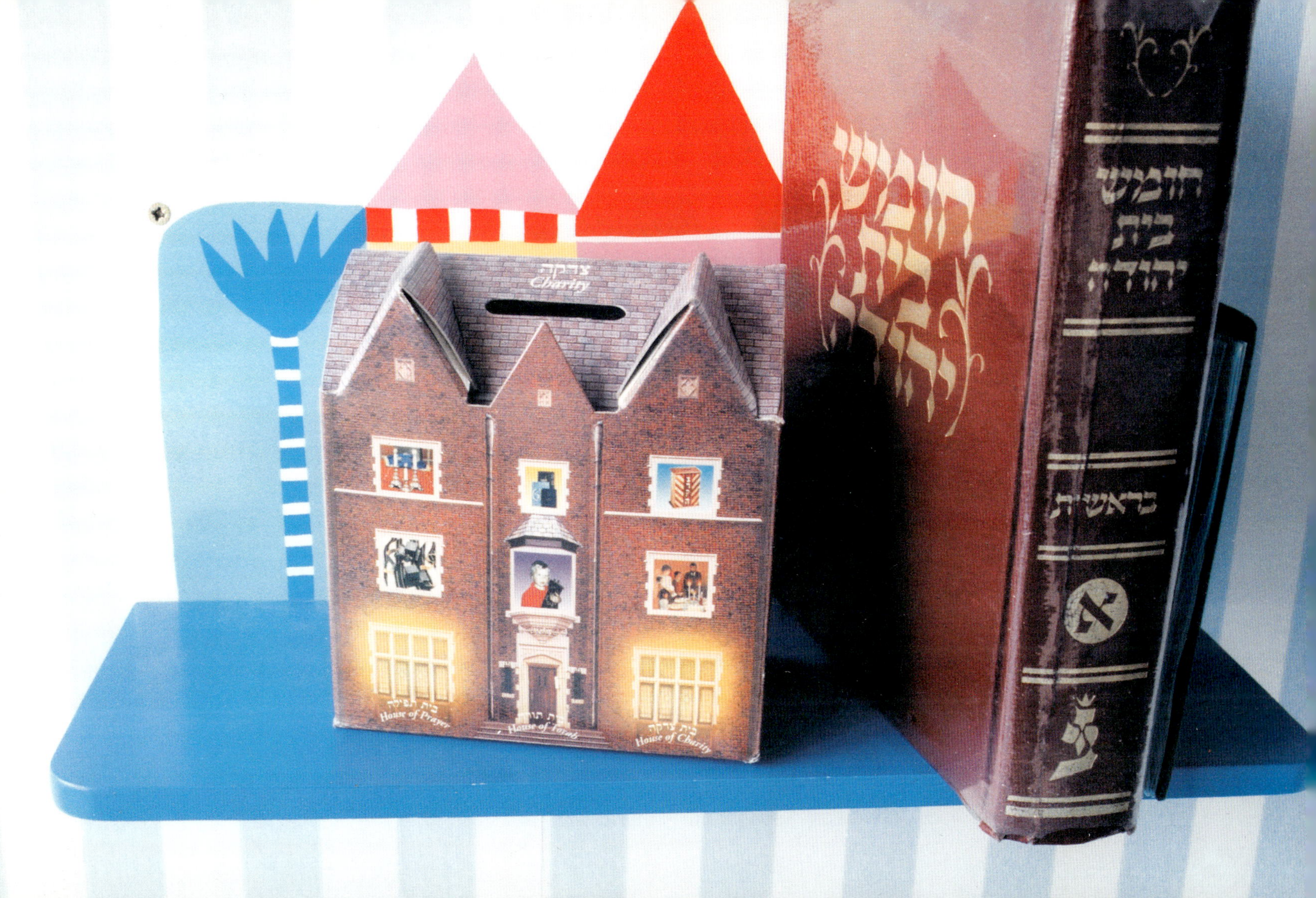
צדקה
Charity
בית תפילה
House of Prayer
בית תורה
House of Torah
בית צדקה
House of Charity
חומש בית יהודה
בראשית

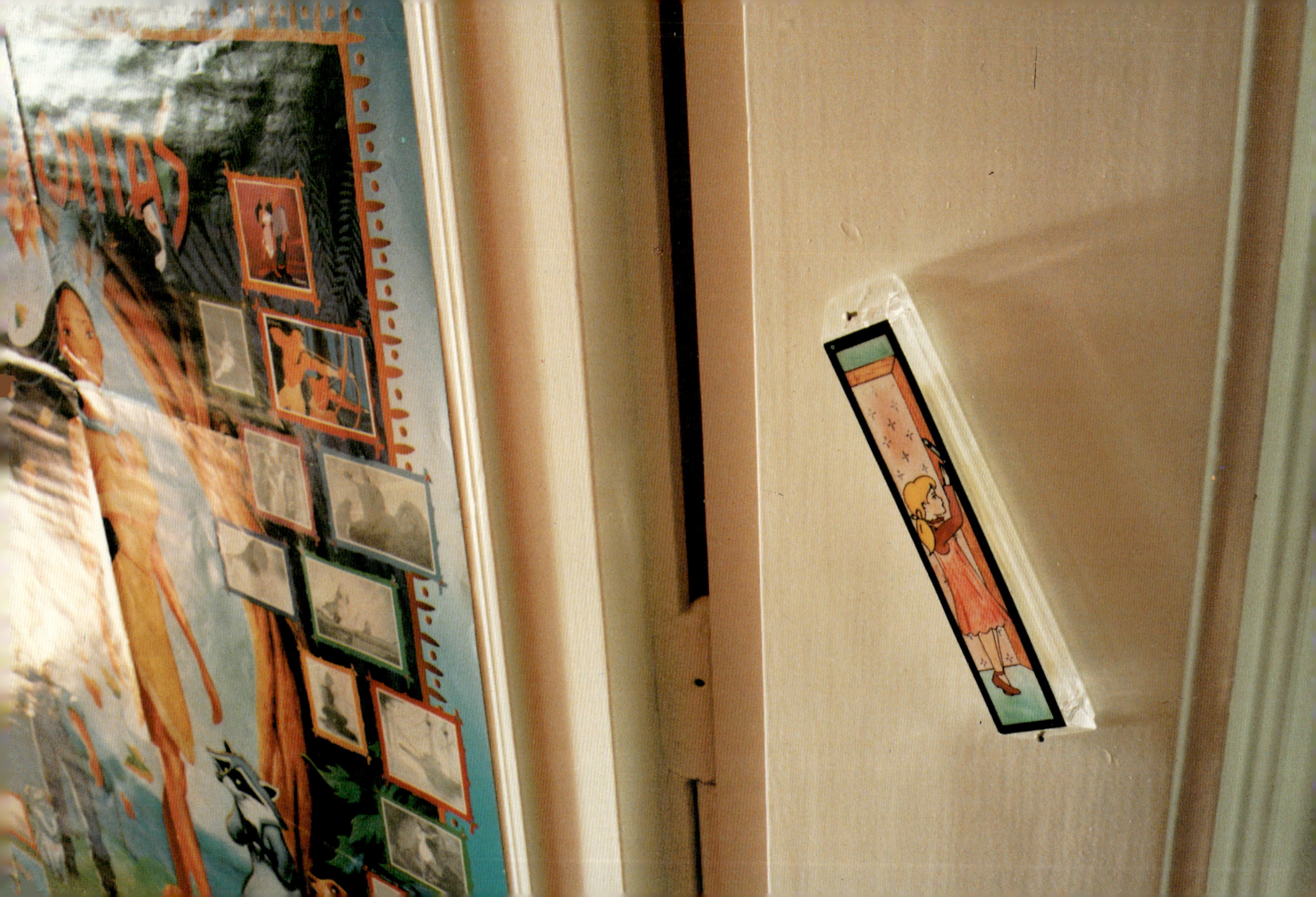

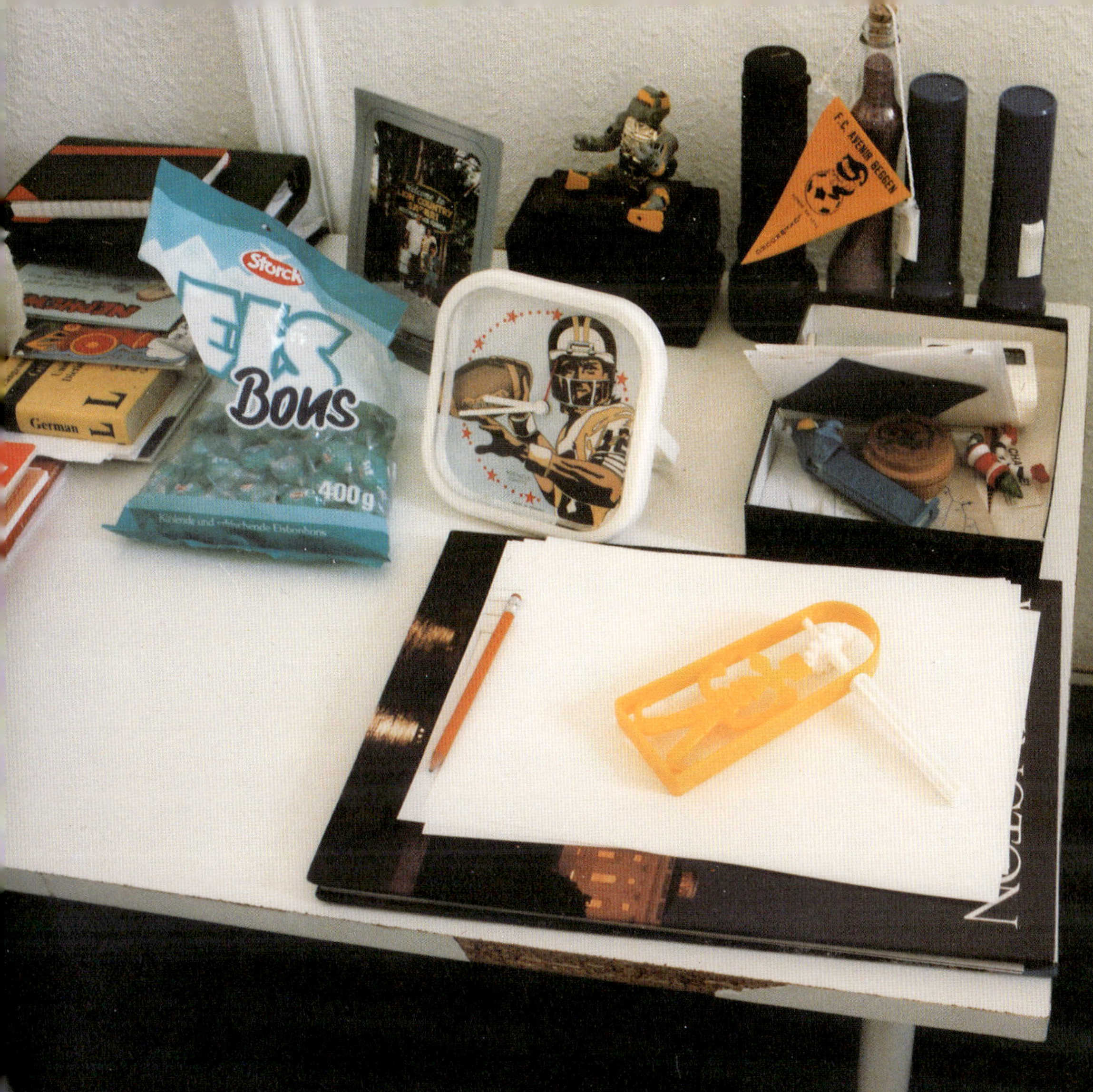

Storch
EIS
Bons
400g
Kühlende und erfrischende Eisbonbons
German
F.C. AVENIR BEGGEN
FESTE DER VÖ
STADT FRANKFURT AM MAIN

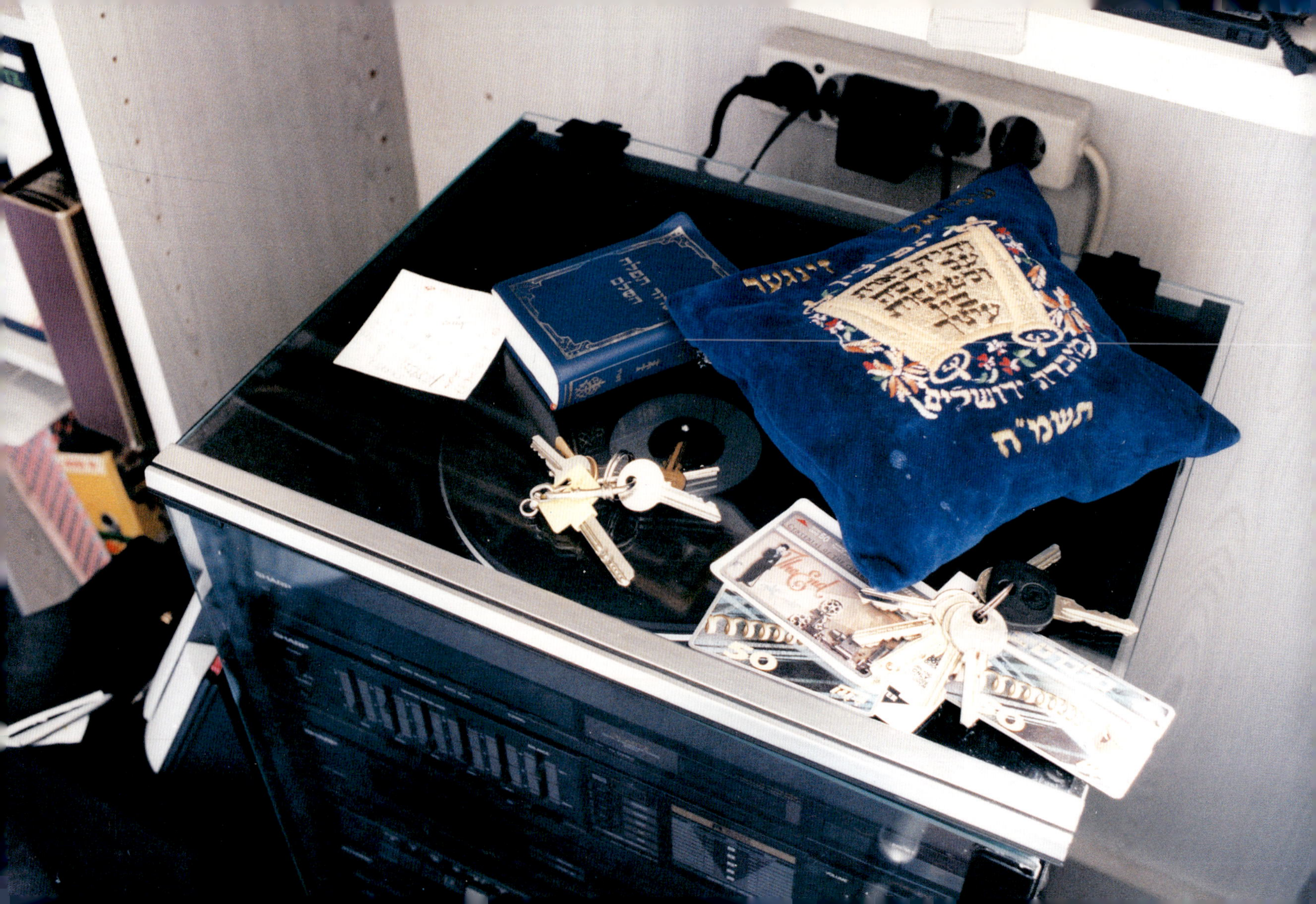

סדור עבודת הלב
מחברת ירושלים
תשמ"ח

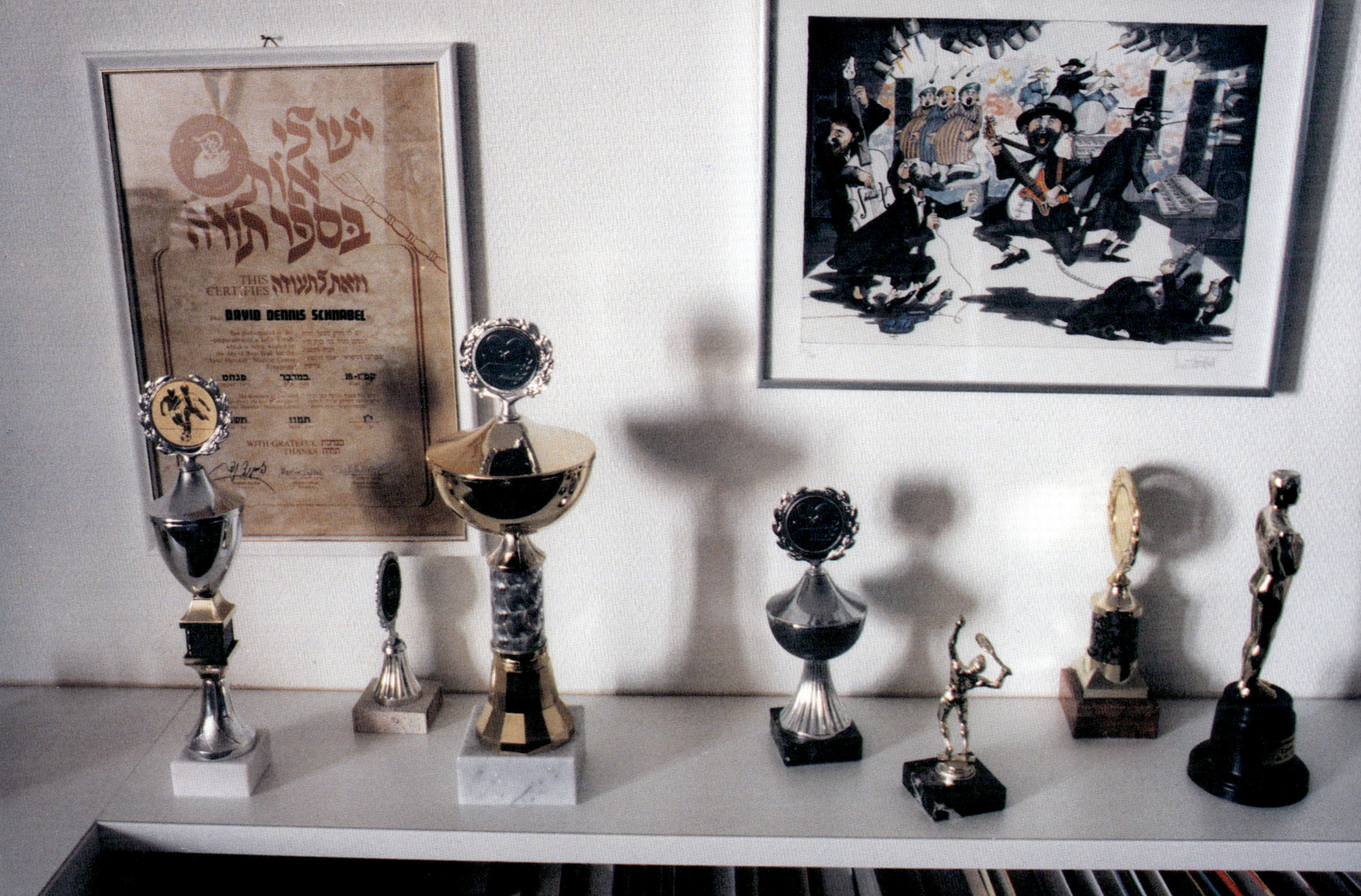

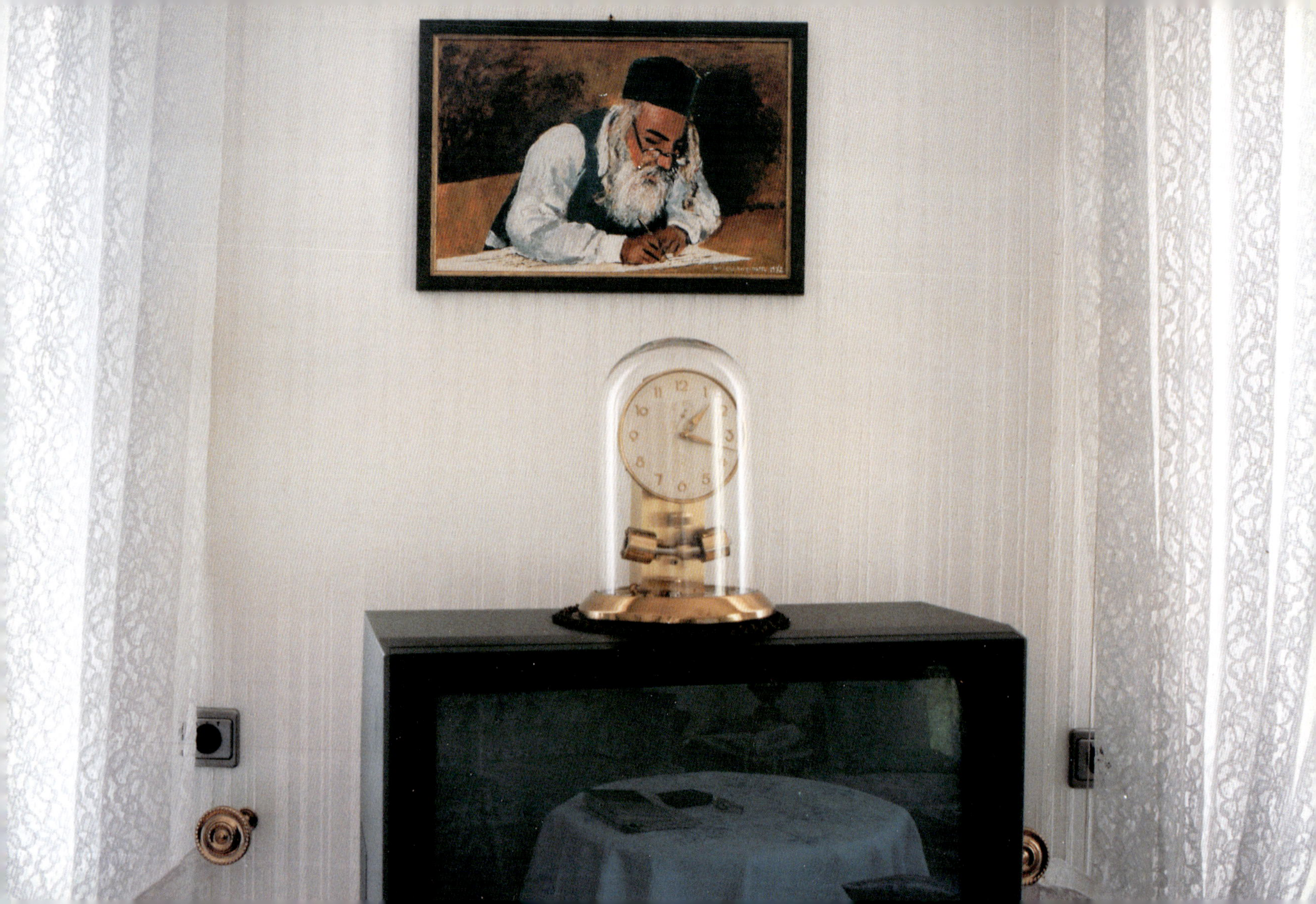

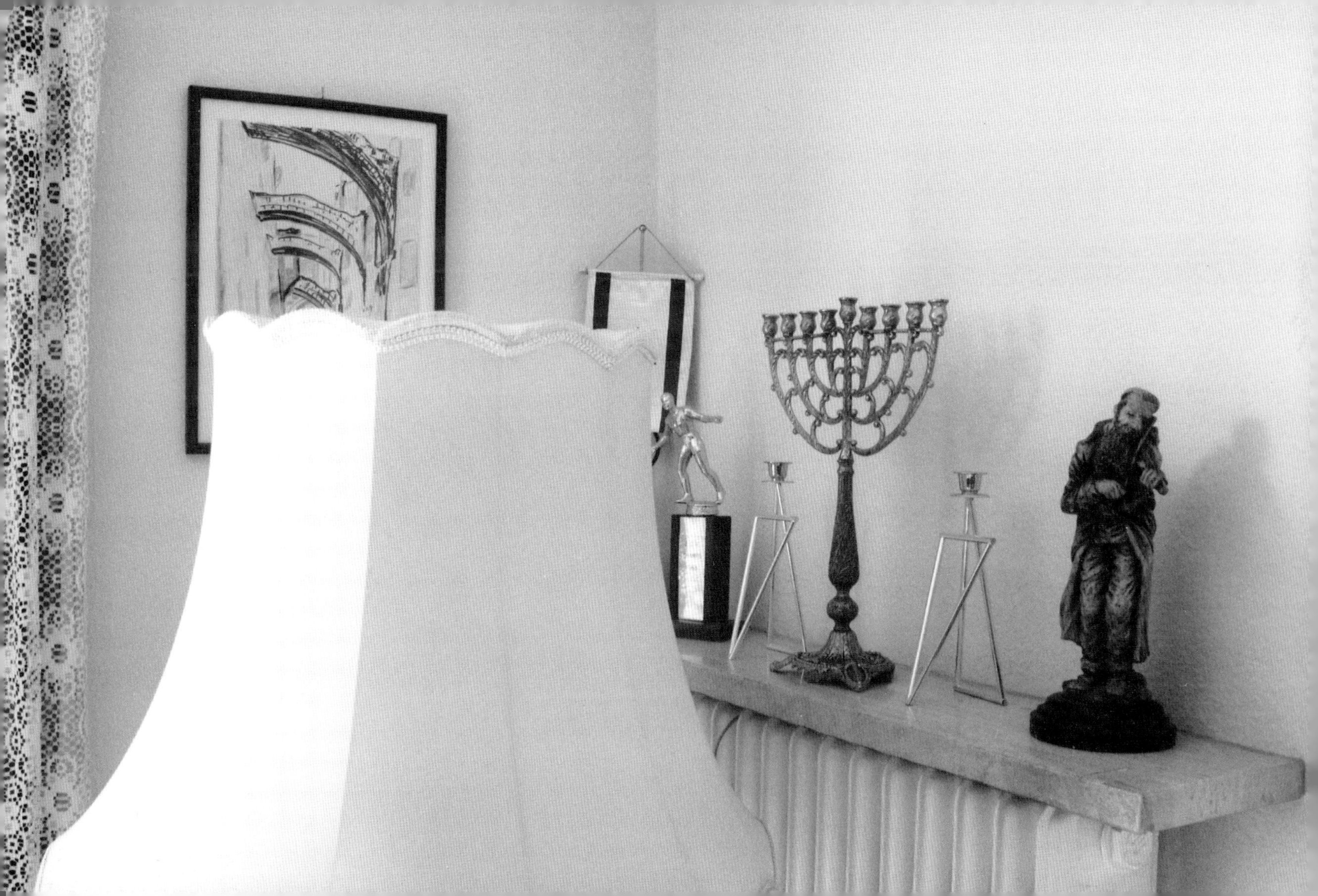

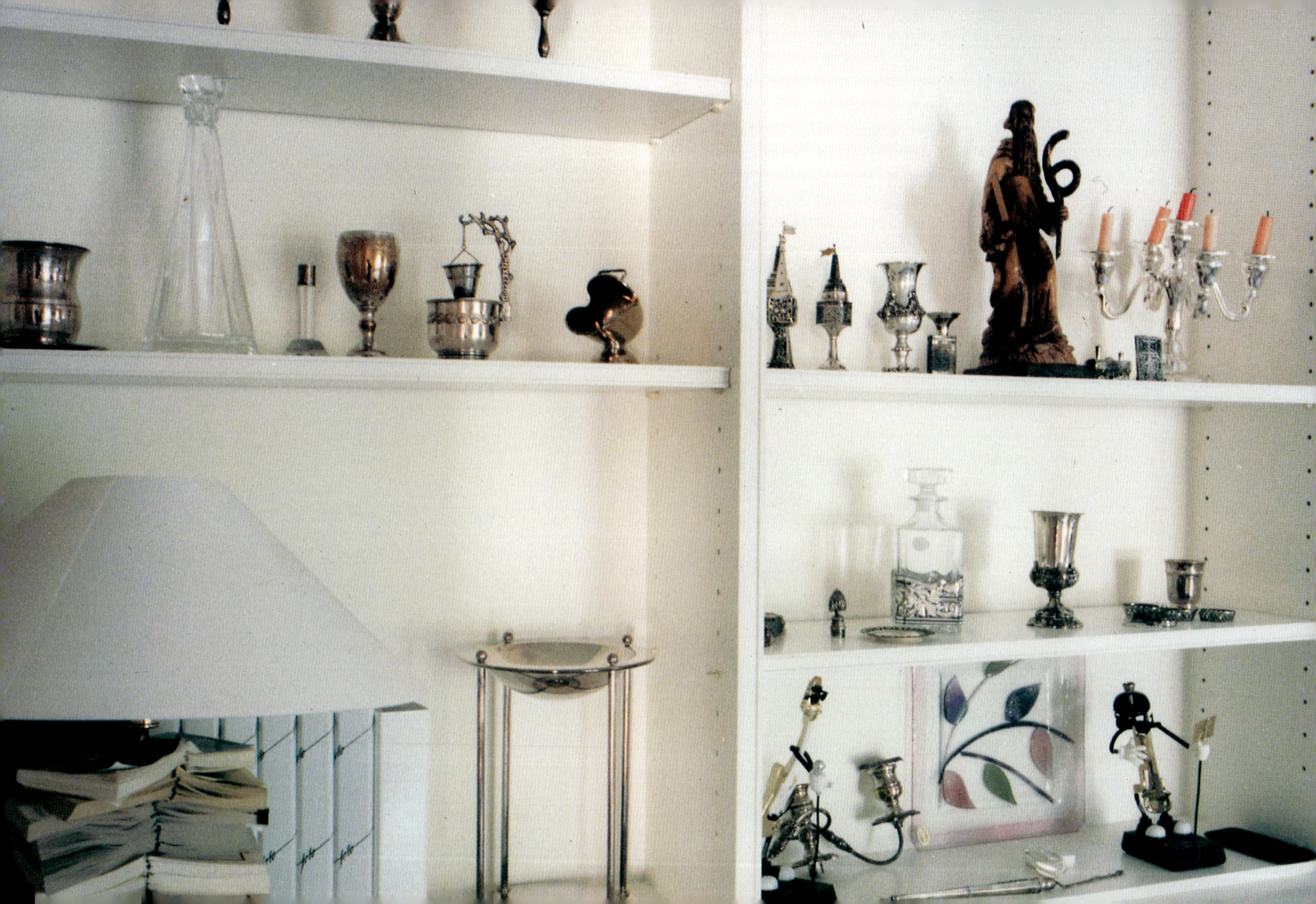

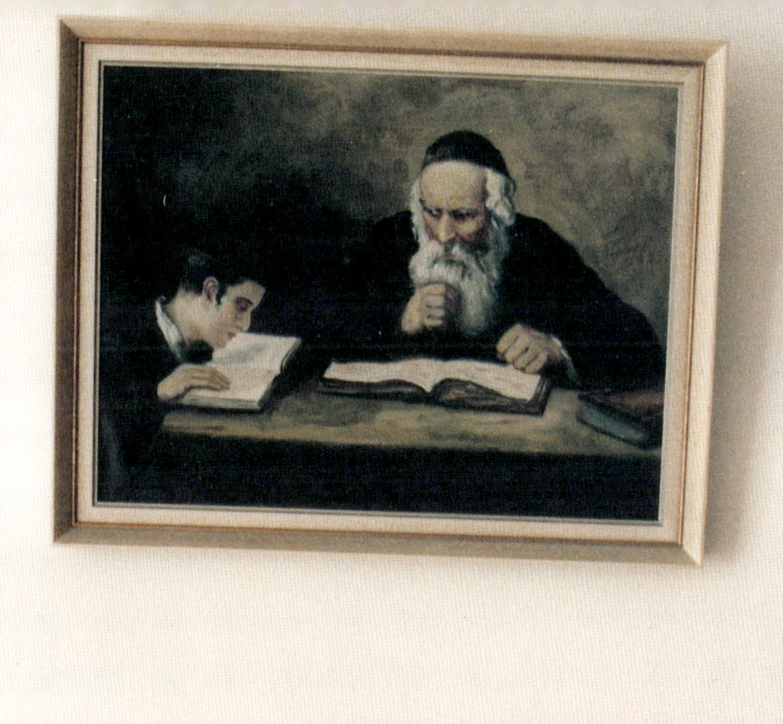
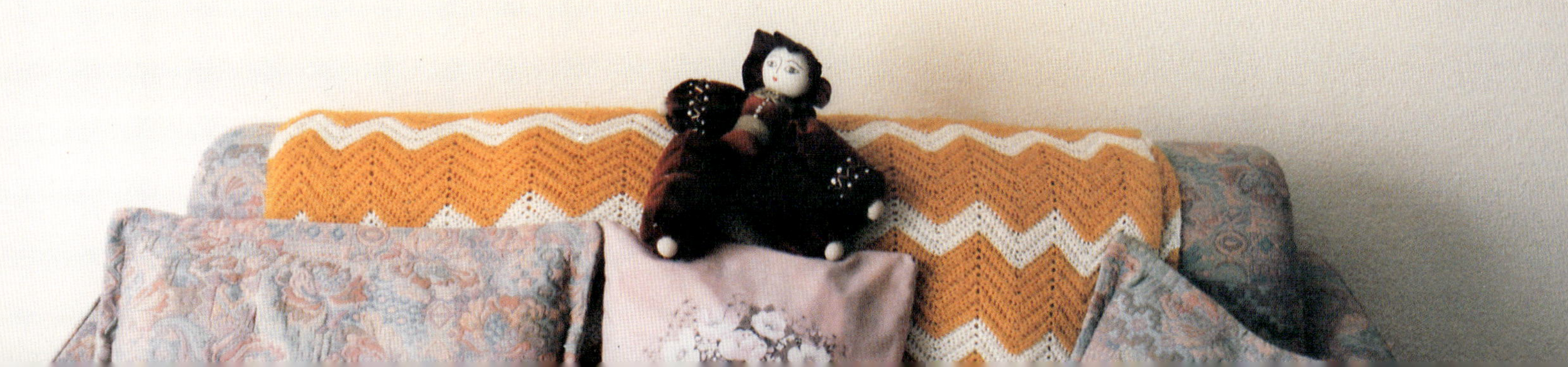

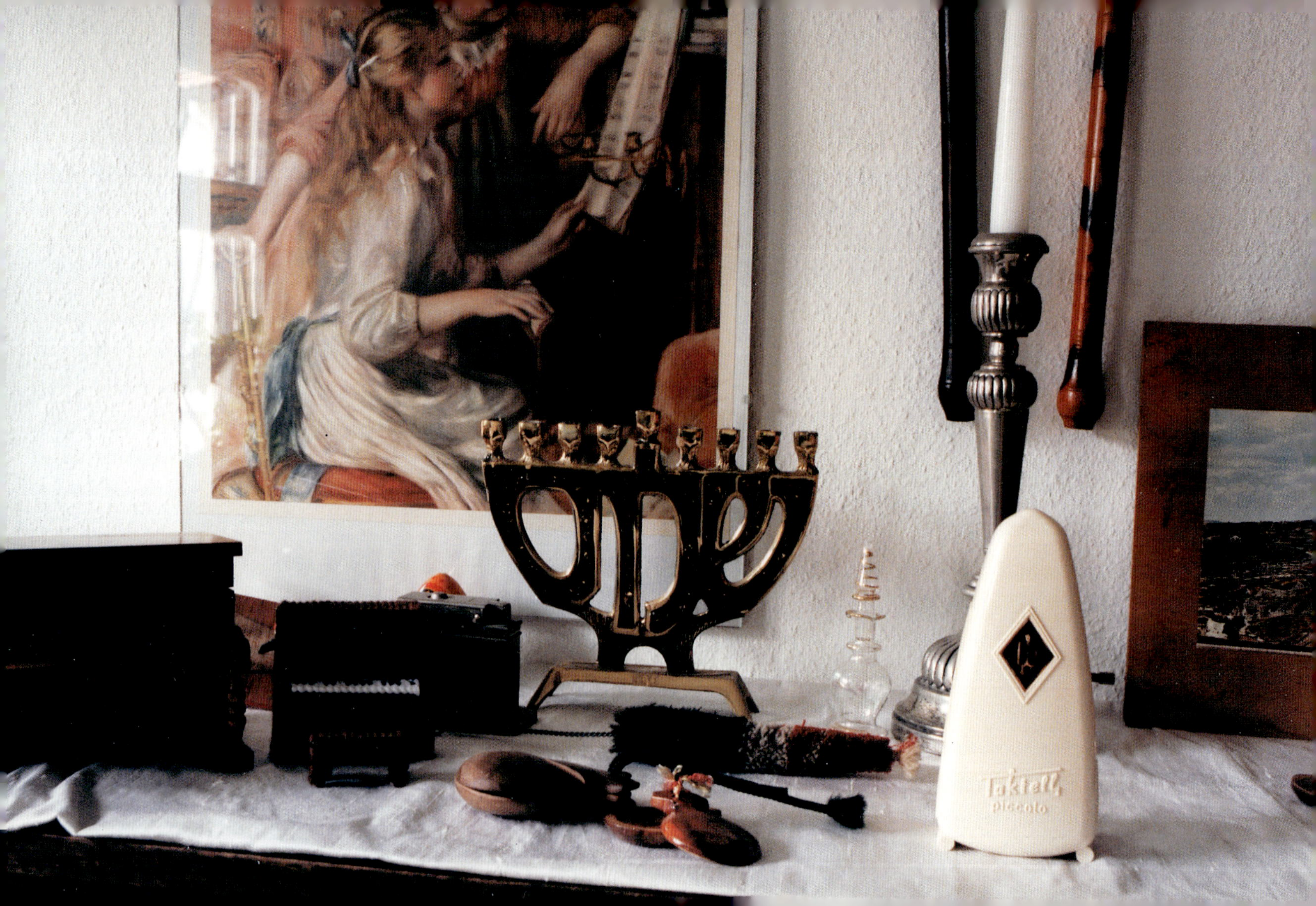
Taktell
piccolo

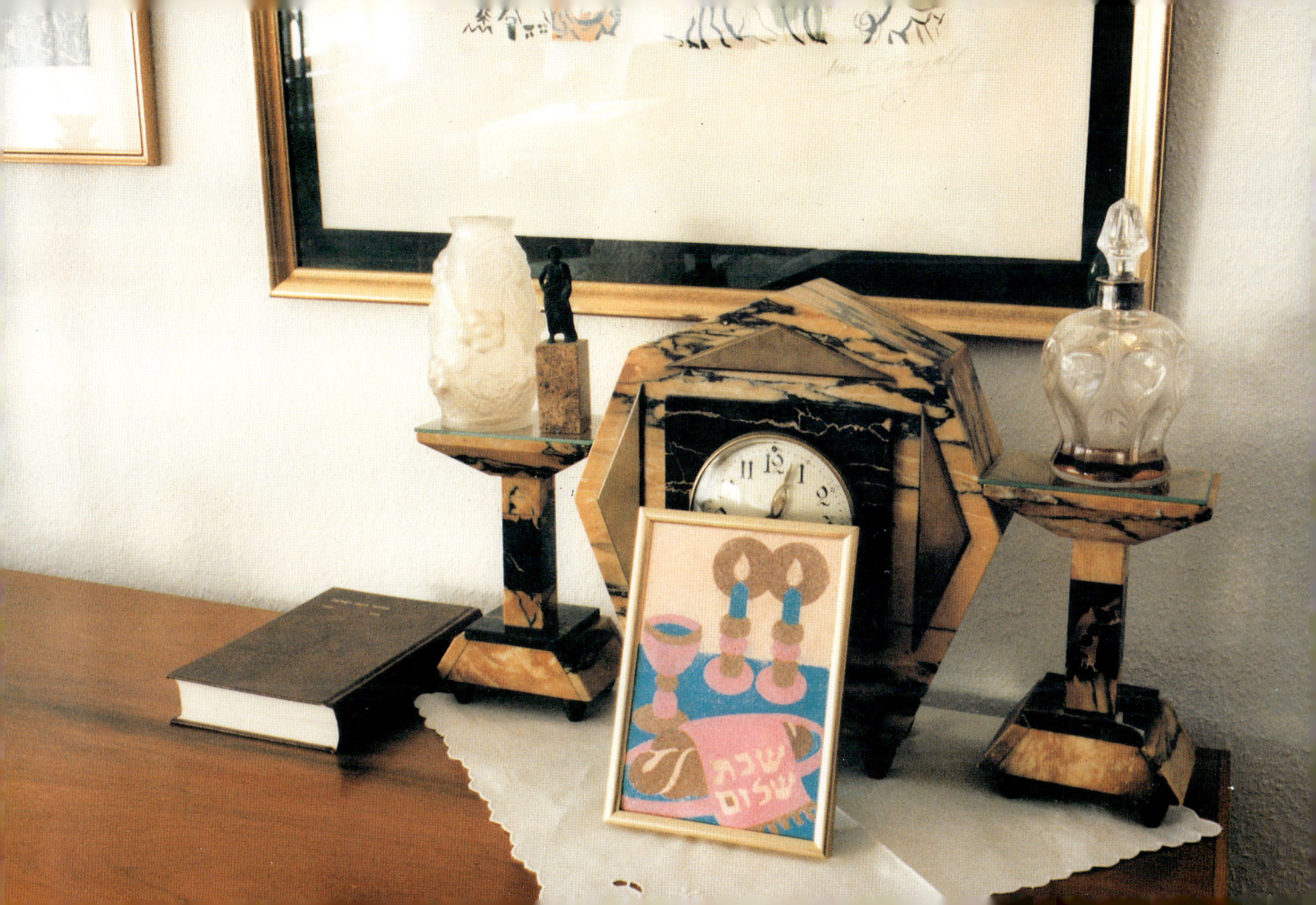

שבת
שלום

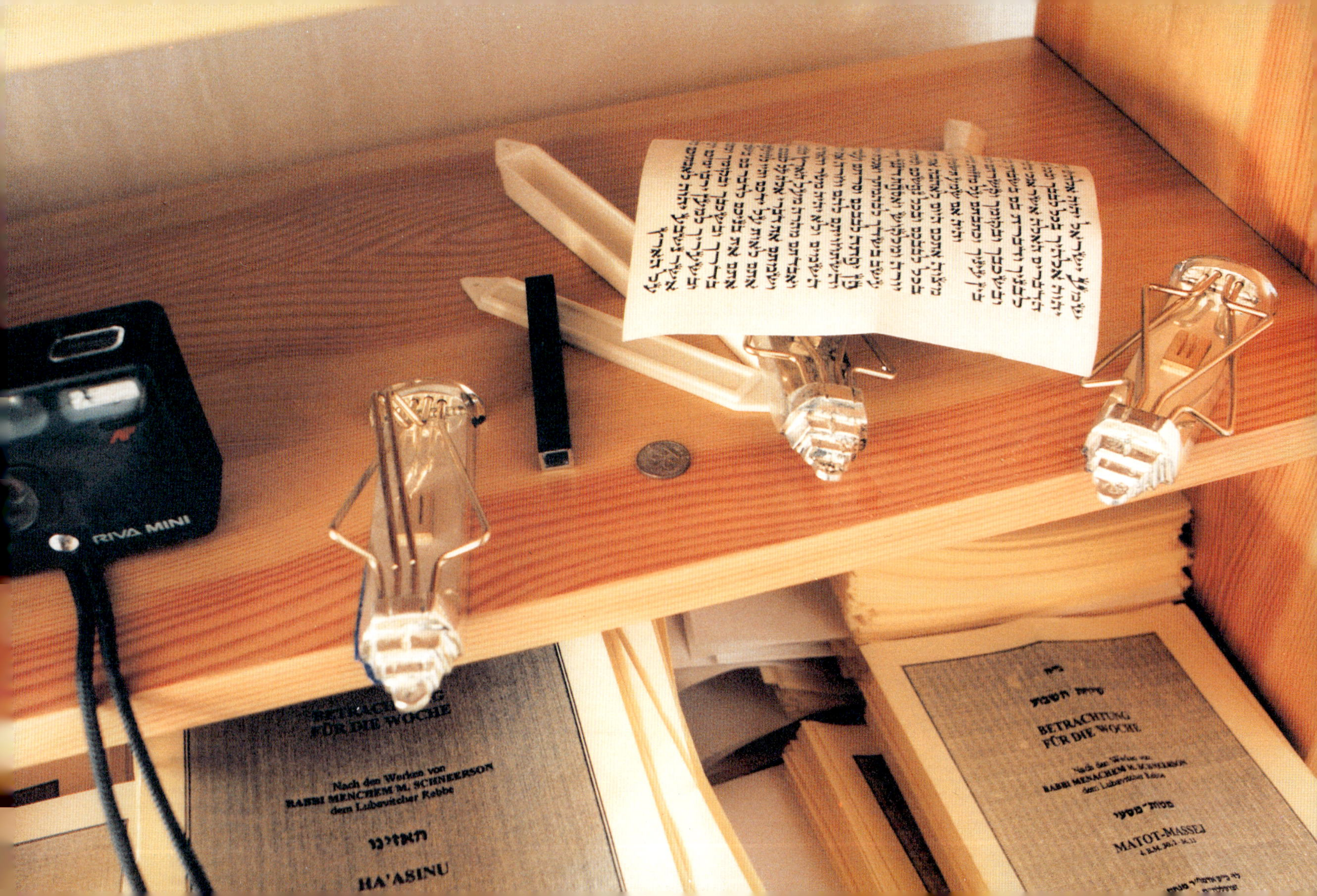
RIVA MINI
BETRACHTUNG FÜR DIE WOCHE
Nach den Werken von
RABBI MENACHEM M. SCHNEERSON
dem Lubawitscher Rebbe
האזינו
HA'ASINU
מטות מסעי
BETRACHTUNG FÜR DIE WOCHE
Nach den Werken von
RABBI MENACHEM M. SCHNEERSON
dem Lubawitscher Rebbe
MATOT-MASSEI
4.BM 30,2 - 36,13

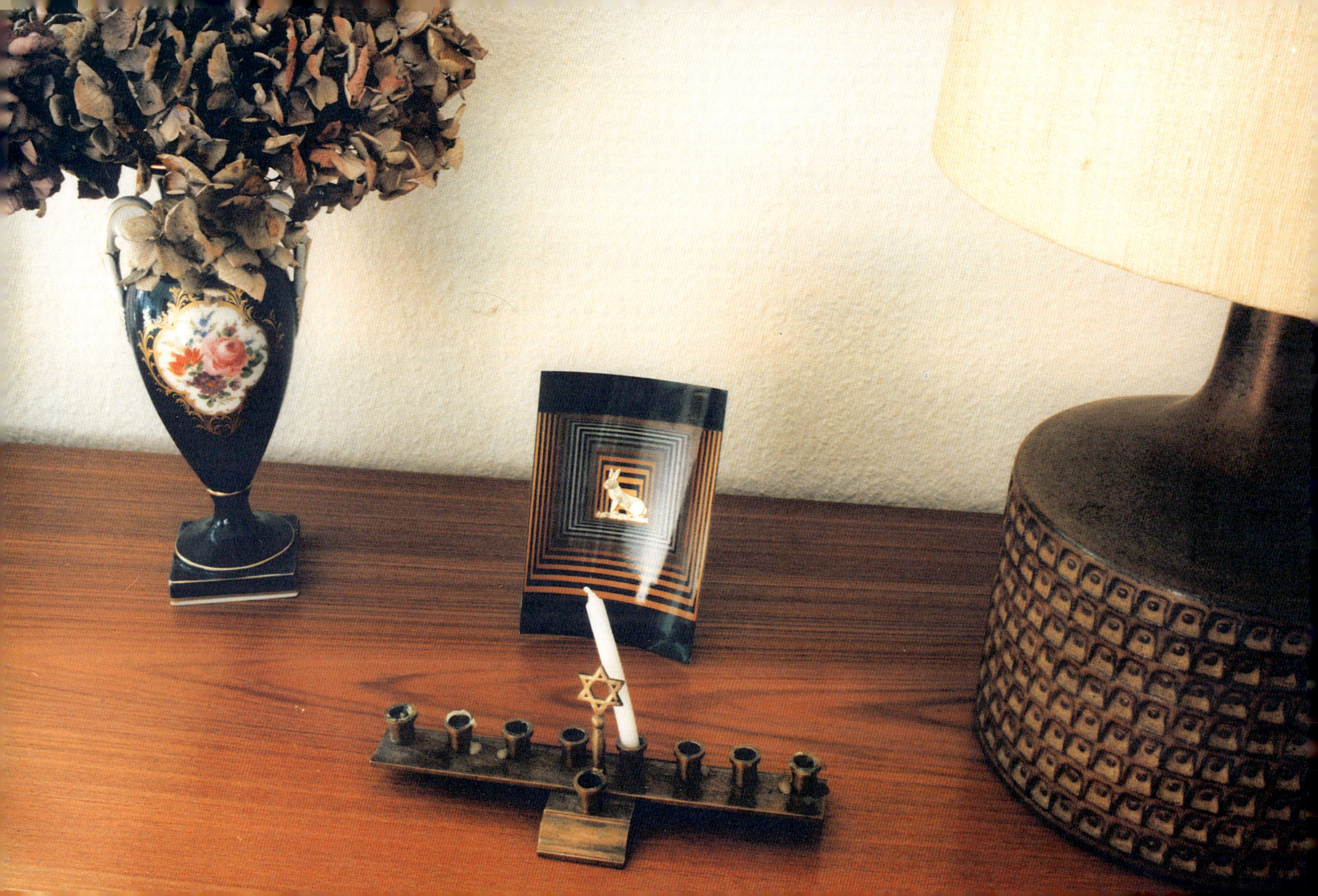

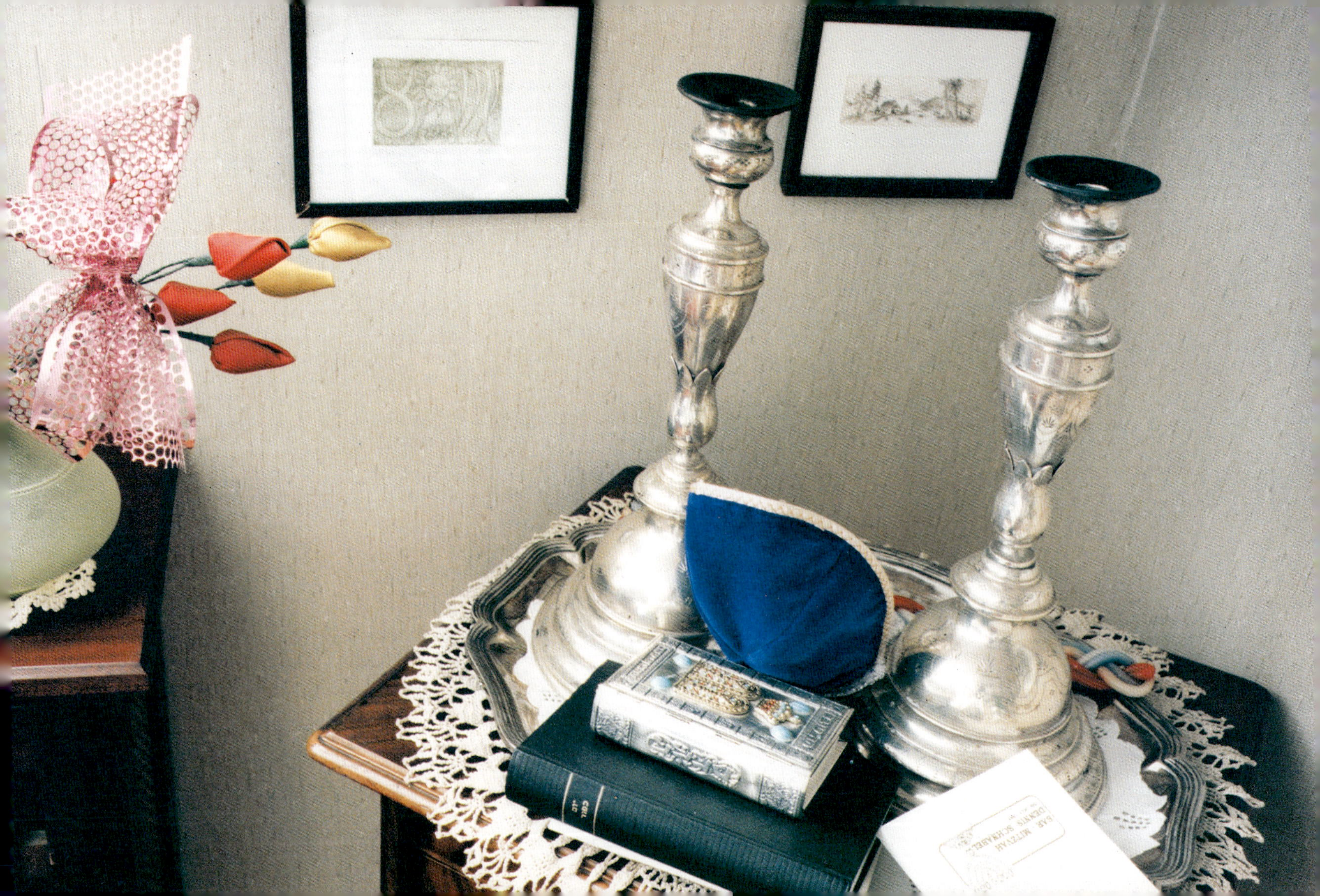
BAR MITZVAH
DENNIS SCHWABEL

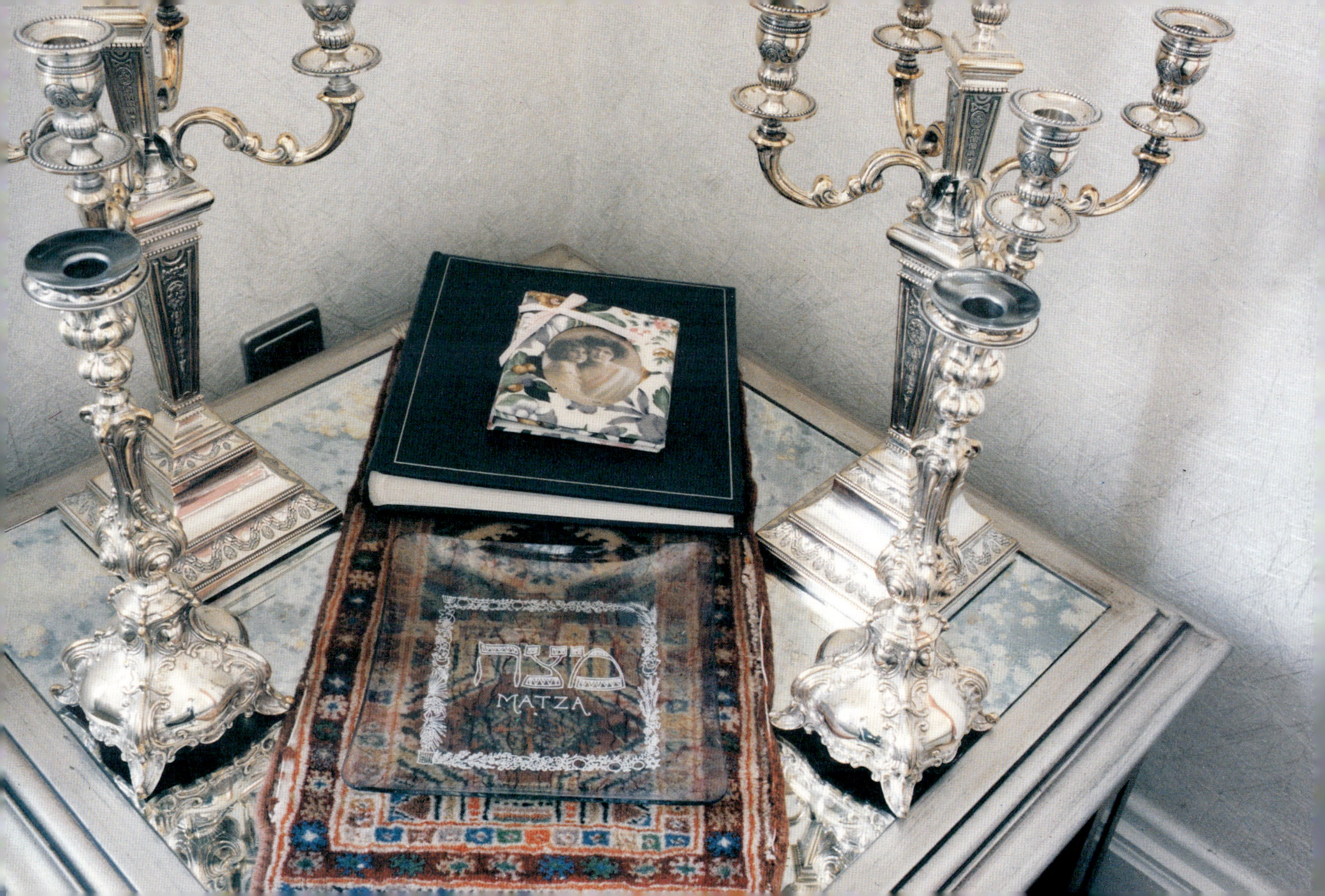

מצה
MATZA

Peter Loewy extends his heartfelt thanks for their trust and kindness

to all those who allowed his gaze into their homes:

The Ackermanns, the Ajnwojners, the Arensteins, Michal Azmon,

Mrs and Mr Bubis, Daniel Cohn-Bendit, Mrs and Mr Engelstein, the Foudims, Esther Friedman,

Michel Friedman, Mrs and Mr Gatterer, the Gurevitchs, Petra and Siggi Guterman,

the Kaffeesieders, Susanna Keval, Rabbi Menahem Halevi Klein, the Knoblochs, the Korens,

Janusch Kozminski, Nili and Matti Kranz, the Lieberbergs, Noam Leslau,

the Majercziks, Tamara Mandel, the Melers, Minka Pradelski, the Reichs, Hannah Salomon,

Mr Sandberg, the Schnabels, the Singers, the Staszewskis,

Mrs and Mr Stoupel, Annette Weber, Mrs Werzberger, Lea Wolff,

his brother Hanno and his parents.

He thanks Cilly Kugelmann for the stimulating conversations

during which the ideas in this book emerged.

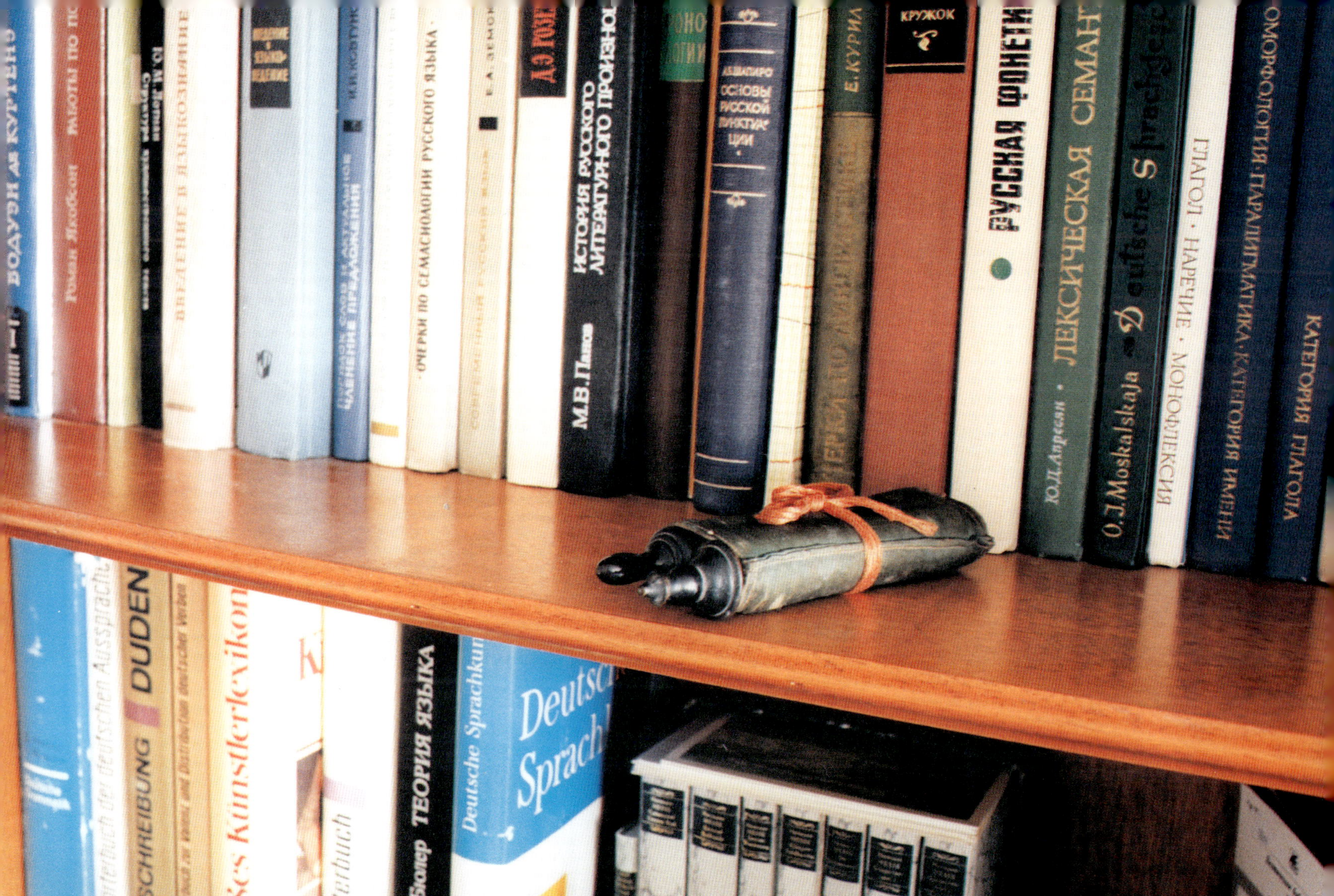

ISBN 3-929078-47-3